D0914036

A BELIEVING JEW

A Believing Jew

THE SELECTED WRITINGS OF

MILTON ⌊STEINBERG⌋

Essay Index Reprint Series

BOOKS FOR LIBRARIES PRESS
FREEPORT, NEW YORK

INTERNATIONAL STANDARD BOOK NUMBER:
0-8369-2256-5

LIBRARY OF CONGRESS CATALOG CARD NUMBER:
76-152215

PRINTED IN THE UNITED STATES OF AMERICA

FOR MY SONS

JONATHAN

AND

DAVID JOEL

PREFATORY NOTE

~~~~~~

THE compiling of this book has been a difficult task on personal grounds. My husband, Rabbi Milton Steinberg, of the Park Avenue Synagogue of New York City died on March 20, 1950 at the age of forty-six. He left behind him the legacy not only of an unforgettable personality, but of considerable literary material—in the form of essays, sermons, and addresses—which constitutes, in its totality, a mirror of his views and his attitude toward life and death. Though much of the material in outline form could not be used for publication, a large and representative section was completely written. The requests of countless friends, added to my own inner compulsion, are responsible for my putting his spoken words into tangible form in this first posthumous volume, *A Believing Jew*.

I was guided in my selections by my knowledge of what my husband held to be important, and I accept full responsibility for the choice. Very little has been changed from the original form. The task of editing and rearranging was undertaken by Maurice Samuel as a gesture of friendship and reverence toward one whom he considered the foremost

7

Rabbinic figure of his generation. I wish to express to him my deepest thanks for rendering so invaluable a service. I also wish to thank Professor Albert Salomon and Rabbi Gerson D. Cohen, who lent their scholarly talents to the reading of the completed book. Finally, I should like to emphasize the fact that all the opinions of Milton Steinberg contained in this book are his personal judgments; they are not to be identified in any form with particular institutions or organizations.

EDITH A. STEINBERG

CONTENTS

9

CONTENTS

I

THE IDEA OF GOD

CHAPTER I

GOD AND THE WORLD'S END

❊❊❊❊❊❊❊❊❊❊❊❊❊❊❊❊❊❊❊❊❊❊❊❊❊❊❊❊❊❊❊❊

THE CHALLENGE to the God faith assails me on all sides.
It shrieks at me from the radio and the headlines of
newspapers. It stirs, like an uneasy presence, in after-dinner
conversation, not the less earnest because it is enunciated
with polite reserve. I see it lurking in the eyes of my con-
gregants, sometimes as a flash of impatience, sometimes as
an anguished, unspoken hope that in me there may reside
a wisdom which shall make the tragedy of our age intelligible, and somehow compatible with the doctrine we pro-
fess together. On occasion, it flares into open, passionate
reproach. The clergy is accused of clinging to a position
which experience has demonstrated to be untenable. And
if anger throbs through the charge, it is the indignation
of a trust that feels itself betrayed.

It is, then, variously expressed, this affront to my inmost
essential belief. But no matter where and in what manner
it manifests itself, even indeed when it fails to become
vocal at all, its purport is the same. How, in the presence
of the vast misery of mankind, the slaughter of innocents,
the staggering stupidity and irrationality of human be-

havior, the victories of brutality and lust, and the complacent tolerance of the scheme of things toward all these, is it possible to believe in God?

From one point of view there is nothing new in the question. The necessity of justifying the ways of God to man is as old as the God idea itself. The inquiries addressed to faith today are, except in scope and intensity, akin to those asked by the prophets and suffering mankind in all its generations. But differences of degree are significant. Between the tickling of the fine point of a pin brushed across the skin, and the sharp flash of pain when metal plunges into the flesh, there is only a difference of degree. But anyone who has been stabbed knows he has not been tickled. It is no personal, private sorrow which now cries for explanation, but the universal agony of mankind, and not merely a present evil, but the threat of greater evils yet to come.

Besides, large moral issues are manifestly involved in the critical struggles of our time. Perhaps the right in all its purity is not all on one side, nor the wrong on the other. Yet there would appear to be at least a preponderance of truth, freedom, and compassion with one set of the antagonists. Of these values, religion has made much. Of them it has asserted that they represent the will of God, and as such are both the way to salvation and, in the long run, invincible in human affairs. The evidences indicate otherwise. Those who put their trust in keeping their powder dry have seemingly been much wiser than those who reposed it in God and a moral order. The issue, then, is twofold. Why should evil be at all, and why should it be so strong against decency and morality?

14

From such problems the atheist is exempt. As he sees it, the whole universe is no more than the purposeless interplay of matter and energy. In its blindness, it is altogether indifferent to man's aspirations, completely insensitive to what he has defined as right and wrong. If events turn out immorally, there is no occasion for perplexity since, after all, the scheme of things is both irrational and unmoral. Herein is to be discerned what may well be the only advantage of atheism. It need not trouble itself with the riddle of theodicy.

But for the religious mind the issue is acute. For it is the essence of faith that behind or above the Many and the Phenomenal stands God, that God is Spirit, that is to say, Reason and Moral Will, and that the world of things and men, since it is an outward expression of Him, must partake of His nature. But if God be, then irrationality and evil ought not be. Yet, they are. Can it be then that God is not?

This is the misgiving which haunts the hearts of millions who believe and half-believe. It presents a challenge with which as a matter of honor, duty, and elemental self-concern religion must come to grips.

II

It was John Stuart Mill who pointed out that no proposition is disproved until it has been refuted in its best form. By the same token, the paradox of evil in a God-motivated universe cannot be said to have been fairly propounded unless both the God faith and the phenomena which seem to deny it are adequately stated, the former in its most mature shape, the latter with maximal realism.

In other words, there is no sense in trying to talk the problem away by denying the reality of evil. Embarrassed theists have from time to time sought escape along this path. They have argued that evil is nothing in itself, that it is only the absence of the good. Or alternatively they have insisted that ugliness, wrong, and irrationality are actually errors of delusions of thought. They have even contended that evil is in some dark and mysterious fashion a good.

Now, to be sure, it is true that, in a sense, all evil is a lack of some desirable condition, that all pain is subjective in character, and we are sometimes better off for having suffered. But this transparently is not the whole story. The question remains: Why? Why should reality be deficient? Why should we be so ordered as to be capable of such egregious mistakes of judgment? The device of verbalizing the dilemma out of existence is then not good enough as a matter of logic. It does not make experience intelligible, which is the very purpose of reason. It is even worse in practice. For the victim of tragic circumstances is not only no further along in understanding his misfortune: he is told that it is not as grievous as he imagines, that he is himself, by his thought processes, the creator of it! Or that the cosmos thus conferred on him a blessing in disguise by subjecting him to torture. Who would dare offer such solace to a mother whose child has been smashed to bits by a bomb, or to a man rotting in a concentration camp for no other offense than his unselfish devotion to the best interests of mankind?

But if one term of the equation must be stated in all its grimness and actuality, the other ought correspondingly to be presented in its clearest, most sober expression. God is variously conceived. In the same congregation different persons confessing the same creed will mean radically different things when they invoke His name. There will be those whose notions are childish, confused, unreasoned; others whose ideas are lucid, tempered by reflection, and refined through criticism. By the former, God will be pictorialized naïvely, perhaps as a patriarch who, seated on a celestial throne and surrounded by angelic hosts, supervises the affairs of the cosmos with unerring sight and by means of direct miraculous intervention. Such a conceit—it cannot justly be called a conception—is, incidentally, by no means limited to the religious. Many an atheist, no better informed, visualizes God in just this fashion, so that his atheism amounts to no more than this: he does not believe in the existence of an old man in the sky.

Now in a free society, every person has the right to any theological opinions he prefers, no matter how crude and primitive. Yet there is an ethic of thought as of behavior, in the light of which man is under the obligation to strive after clarity and purity of idea. A second-best religious understanding is therefore a violation of the moral code of the intellect. At the same time, it cannot possibly be equal to the large issues which it is called on to make comprehensible. Nowhere is this truth more vividly exhibited than in the matter which concerns us here. For an immature God conception can offer interpretations of evil only on its own level. Since God is a glorified man, His actions must be interpreted anthropomorphically. Either, then, He is being wanton and capricious with His world, or else he is fulfilling some mysterious design known only to Him. In either case, we are denied understanding of our experiences. Our quest for insight is frustrated. We must content ourselves with the sorry, unprofitable thought that while what befalls us seems to make nonsense, it does have meaning to God. But since one of the major functions of religious faith is to render life intelligible, the whole enterprise ends by defeating itself.

Yet, even on the plane of the sophisticated and philosophical, God is variously conceived. No sooner, therefore, do we grant that any significant theodicy must be drawn in terms of a fully ripened theism, then the issue arises, which theism? Now if we were concerned here with an exhaustive treatment of our subject, we would proceed to an examination of every God idea and of the manner in which each deals with the issue before us. But our present purpose will be better served by the presentation of a specimen position. To this end I offer, as the *corpus vile* of an experiment in the reconciliation of the world with God, the theology I know best and most intimately—my own.

It is not the only acceptable theism. God, as the reality of all realities, will inevitably overflow any set of concepts and all the concepts which man can fashion to capture His essence. Alternative constructions of God must be forever possible; considering the same Being, different men will, according to their individual capacities and points of departure, catch different aspects of it.

Nor do I pretend that there is anything radically novel

in my viewpoint. Quite the contrary. Its antecedents are ancient, honorable, and a matter of public record. The student of philosophy will readily detect in it traces of Bergson and Hegel, the neo-Platonic *Logos*, the Stoic *Pneuma*, the Rabbinic *Shekinah* and *Memra*. What is more, it is, except for certain minor details which may be peculiar to me, representative of a large segment of contemporary religious opinion.

But just because it is not advanced as the only possible theology, just because it is neither original nor unique, it is all the better capable of serving as a trying-ground on which the God faith in one fairly typical form can be tested as to its tenability in the presence of evil.

III

The entire universe, as I see it, is the outward manifestation of Mind-Energy, of Spirit, or to use the older and better word, of God. God is then the essential Being of all beings, though all beings in their totality do not exhaust Him. It is His reason which expresses itself in the rationality of nature, in the fact that all things behave in conformity with intelligible forms, in the fact, in brief, that the world is cosmos not chaos. His power moves in the dynamisms of physical reality. His will is the impulse behind the upsurge of life on this planet. Individualized, He is the soul of man whose thought processes are infinitesimal sparks of His infinite fire, whose moral aspirations are fragments of His vast purpose, whose yearning to create is but an echo of His cosmic creativity. And He is an ethical being, not so much in the sense that He enters into relations with His own expressions, as in the deeper sense that He is the fountainhead, source, and sanction of man's moral life. The human quest after freedom, truth, goodness, and beauty is but the splintered spearhead of the divine drive. So to me, the whole panorama of earth and sky, the tempestuous progress of living things, the tortuous career of humanity are the external shell of a process wherein God realizes His character.

Such is my faith. Yet, no sooner do I state it than a large question arises which is both legitimate in itself and, as we shall see, relevant to the matter at hand: On what in reason and experience does my affirmation rest? In another age, I would have answered simply: On faith. And men would have understood. They would have known at once that I was affirming a proposition which could not be altogether proved but for the acceptance of which sufficient reason existed. But the word faith has to the modern ear acquired unhappy and derogatory overtones. It is charged, even for thoughtful persons who should know better, with connotations of intellectual laziness, obscurantism, and even perverse attachment to the irrational. I shall then employ a term which means substantially the same thing but whose flavor is more acceptable to the modern palate. I shall assert that my God belief is a hypothesis, interpreting the universe as a whole.

But if it is only a faith or hypothesis, it is not one which I have adopted wantonly. Rather have I been driven to it by compelling considerations. I affirm it, first, because this seems to me to be the only theory which accounts for reality as I know it in personal experience and as science describes it. Here before me unfolds a universe which is dynamic, creative, and rational in the sense that everything in it conforms to the law of its own being, a world that has produced in living things what seems to be purposiveness and in man the phenomenon of consciousness. No other theory except that which posits a Thought-Will as the essence of things fits such a scene.

I believe as I do, furthermore, because of the practical necessities of human existence. To live well men need joy and hope concerning their destiny and courage in facing it. They require, moreover, a sense of their own worth and of the significance of the lives of their fellows. Without such convictions, the ethical life is bankrupt at its source. There will exist justification neither for self-realization nor for self-sacrifice. Against the requirements of man's morale and morality, only the theistic outlook is adequate, for it alone assures him that life adds up to sense rather than nonsense, that it is design rather than a succession of chance syllables in a cosmic idiot's tale.

And of all possible interpretations of reality, this is the simplest. Given the one God concept, the whole universe bursts into lucidity. The rationality of nature, the emergence of life, the phenomena of conscience and consciousness become intelligible. Deny it and the whole becomes inexplicable. There is then a kind of esthetic neatness about the religious position. It is marked by that economy of idea which is one of the goals of all inquiry.

Superior plausibility, practicality, and simplicity—these are the grounds on which my God postulate rests. I admit freely that I have not demonstrated my position fully and beyond dispute. But I know also that no proposition, no matter of what character, can be established beyond the possibility of challenge, that every judgment of reason, including those of the sciences, inductive and deductive alike, is either postulate or derived from and shot through with it. The limitations in my case are but the universal limitations of the intellect.

What is more, it is on the basis of these very considerations—plausibility, practicality, and simplicity—that the scientist posits *his* hypotheses. The religious affirmation, in other words, is no unique and unparalleled enterprise. It is but an application to the business of interpreting reality-as-a-whole of a technique general to reason. So long then as one refrains from the attempt to construe the cosmos, or refuses arbitrarily to employ to that end the normal processes of thought, he can avoid the God concept. But so soon as he undertakes to comprehend what lies behind the face of things and thinks systematically on that issue as he thinks on others, the God faith becomes well-nigh inescapable.

IV

And still evil remains.

We have contended that the God concept is the only adequate principle of explanation for the universe, that it is, as it were, a solvent in which an obscure and turgid world dissolves into luminosity. But even with God the solution is not altogether clear. Precipitates persist, dark residues that defy liquefaction. The misgiving assails us that our solvent is not good enough, or even that our rationale of religion has been made possible only by a judicious selection of the evidences.

It is an old and tragic paradox which confronts us: the sons of God have assembled and lo, Satan is among them. Are we then trapped in an impasse so that we must forever vacillate between aye and nay? Or is there a way out?

If there is an exit, it most certainly does not consist in rejecting the God-idea. This we have affirmed for valid and sufficient reasons. Let us abandon it and we shall have landed straight from the frying pan into the fire. For if in the light of the theistic scheme we have our difficulties with evil, with the atheistic case we shall have larger and greater troubles. We shall be forced to explain how the blind workings of matter and energy shall have produced a rational world, how the purposiveness of animals and men shall have evolved out of cosmic pointlessness, how human freedom and intelligence shall have been the product of brute mechanical necessity.

Besides—and this is a circumstance which is often overlooked—the evils which seemingly deny God are themselves rational. When a man slips on the ice and breaks his leg, the event is a misfortune to him, but it is not irrational. Indeed, so completely intelligible is it that an osteologist who knew in advance the composition of the bone, the fulcral point and the stress to be brought on it, could have predicted the fracture. So with other calamities of life— avalanches, diseases, manias, these are all comprehensible in reason. The geologist, physician, and psychologist re-

23

spectively, understand them, and find in them not violations but corroboratory instances of scientific law. Whatever emotional protests the experience of evil may evoke in man, whatever moral perplexities it may occasion, it constitutes no affront to his purely intellectualistic insights. The fact that evil itself is not without its logic has suggested to some metaphysicians possible resolution of our riddle. This would consist in affirming God as the rational, that is intelligible, essence of all things but in making of Him an unmoral being. In the history of human speculation, harried and weary theologians recurrently have taken refuge in this device. As an escape from our paradox, it is obviously inadequate. A God who is beyond and unrelated in nature to the categories of good and evil, fails as a principle of explanation of man's soul. He is unequal, pragmatically, to those needs of the human heart which drive men to seek out their deities. Neither in logic nor utility is He enough.

But if, on the one hand, we cannot refuse to take cognizance of evil, if, on the other, we cannot reject God, and if, beyond all these, we cannot dissociate Him from the mishaps, injustices, and anguish of life, then one course, and one course only, remains open to us. We must affirm God boldly and then see what becomes of our dilemma. We must, without in the least minimizing the tragic experiences against which we protest, inquire whether they cannot somehow be made compatible with His existence. Perhaps we shall discover on closer consideration not only that God is denied by evil less sharply than we imagine but also that He illumines it and makes it intelligible.

V

The evils to which we are subject are many and grievous. We are in body the slaves of time, space, and causality. We can be wounded or shattered by the forceful impact of other objects. We are forever beset by invisible enemies who seek to penetrate our defenses and maintain themselves in life by feeding on, and so destroying us, the host organism. We are driven by hunger, thirst, and desire and can die in agony for want of food, water, or air. Worst of all, we are all actually or potentially the victims of the stupidity, cruelty, and rapacity of that most feral of all beasts, man. All the woes of all that is, of the mineral, of the vegetable, of the animal, are ours. If ontogeny recapitulates phylogeny, if the individual reviews in his biological career the history of his race, and his race that of life as a whole, then it would seem that man has carried over into his existence all the disabilities of all the orders of being through which he has passed. And to this catalogue, he has added some items peculiar to himself—an awareness of his distresses, loneliness, bereavement, frustration, and disillusionment.

If there are advantages to being human, there are transparently large and tragic disadvantages as well. Yet, given the scheme of things, it must be so. For man has emerged through, and stands astride the animal, the animal the plant, the plant the mineral. The whole of life is a gigantic acrobatic feat in which the tumblers on top are mounted level after level on the shoulders of those below. The limitations of the nethermost will be those of the uppermost also. Let the one who stands lowest be in a particular place at a particular time and the whole superstructure must be there with him. Let him tremble, and a quiver will pass upward through the entire edifice.

Now mankind at the top of the heap has a character of its own, a nature which from the religious viewpoint is an especially vivid instance of the Spirit behind the whole process. Humanity, theism would say, partakes of Deity and exhibits Him with peculiar distinctiveness. As God is the Reason in all things, so man is capable of thought and of the knowledge of the truth. As He is freedom, creativity, a resident in all souls, and the source of all goodness, so His mortal individualizations yearn after freedom, will to create, strive after insights into other hearts, and aspire after ideal ends. In traits held in common with the divine, the humanity of mankind consists. In the manifestation of them lies its goal. Which is exactly what the old theologians had in mind when they insisted that man exists for the glory of God.

But even as we set forth to fulfill our destiny, in the midst of our realization of it, the conditions of our being remind us forcibly that we are also kin to the mineral and, like it, prisoners of time and space; near relative to the plant and, in consequence, exposed to bacterial attack, hunger, and thirst; blood brother to animals and, like them, engaged in competitive struggle, like them capable of rage, hatred, and bloodlust.

The nature of evil now becomes clear. It is the persistence of the circumstances of lower strata in higher; the carry-over of the limitations of the orders of being on which man's existence is based into his personality and society. It is then a reality, but one that is essentially relativistic. For the factors that offend us are legitimate on their original scene. They are not inherently wrongful; they become such on being translated into other realms. That one stone has broken another appears to us a matter devoid of ethical significance. It is an altogether different story when a stone wounds a human being, for that event prevents his self-fulfillment. We would not say that the sullen ferocity of the gorilla represents an immorality on its part. But we do believe ourselves confronted with sin when man is sullenly ferocious. Childishness, whether of the individual or the species, is after all appropriate to children and to be expected of them. It becomes disturbing only when it persists in grown persons.

So regarded, the whole evolutionary record is the tale of the hangover of restraints. More deeply considered, it is the saga of life's continuous victory over them. The vegetable has transcended the mineral, or it would have remained inorganic; the animal the plant. And as for man, the heritage of the beast is still powerful in him. He can be irrational, cruel, destructive. What more could fairly be expected of so recent an upstart? But already he holds in his hands, though in crude and primitive form, the instruments for continuous ascent: the intellect and skills which shall progressively emancipate him from his bondages, the moral insights and principles which shall subdue what remains of the inner beast.

Now let us put this entire process in religious, rather than naturalistic terms. Let us see indeed whether it is susceptible of such statement. For this is the crux of the matter before us: Is the God hypothesis adequate to account for the whole story of reality, including the unhappy motif of evil that runs through it? Can the solvent which reduced so much to lucidity, dissolve the dark residues also?

The emergence of life, as the theist sees it, is no blind eddy over a directionless stream. It is the progressive incarnation of a cosmic Thought-Will. The Spirit which drives the whole movement is forever involved in its own revelation; and yet forever transcending them. God as He mounts from level to level is, like an embryo bursting forth from the womb, still stained and flecked with the stuff of His immersion. Yet He has no sooner begun to give birth to a new self-manifestation than the traces of the old commence to fall away. Man's inhumanity to man, which troubles us so deeply, is of just such a character. It is, from the religious viewpoint, a caul still firmly fixed to the infant, but destined to be sloughed as under the divine impulse mankind grows to fuller stature.

Our crucial question—Can God be if evil is—has now answered itself. There is nothing in one term which is incompatible with the other. Indeed, under the religious hypothesis, the essential nature of evil becomes explicable. It is the still unremoved scaffolding of the edifice of God's creativity.

Perhaps we would have preferred that it had all been otherwise, that our consciousness, conscience, creativity, and moral freedom had sprung into being full-blown, untrammeled and untroubled by the heritages of lower orders of being. Certainly, even when we accept the scheme of things we are impatient with its slowness, with the irregularity and tardiness in which truth and goodness and liberty rise from out of blindness, bestiality, and bondage. But it is with reality as given that we must deal; of things as they are that we are speaking. To account for the world not as we would like it but as we have it, to strengthen our hearts, not steadfast as we might desire them but frail as they really are—the God faith is an indispensability. And there is nothing in that faith which is controverted either by the fact of evil or the unhurried tempo with which life surmounts it.

VI

It is a long and weary way which our inquiry has led us. And now that we approach its end, it may be pertinent to inquire wherein we are the better off for having undertaken the journey.

We have, to be sure, found an escape from an intellectual impasse. This, indisputably, is something. The solution of any paradox, no matter how academic, is, under any circumstance, a legitimate and worth-while human enterprise. What is more, we have at the least mitigated the contradiction between those factors in our experience which proclaim a God and those which would seem to deny Him. This is even more. For the God idea is one of the most significant in the realm of reason. The vindication of it is an urgent and momentous business.

But evil is more than a concept to be harmonized neatly with others, more than an abstraction about which exercises in logic can be conducted. It represents a grim, fearsome, concrete reality with which every human being who has ever lived has, each in his own fashion, been called upon to deal. The weight of it is especially heavy in this age of travail. Across the seas whole peoples suffer and perish. And we whose destiny is bound up with theirs, who are made one with them through sympathy, carry something of their burdens in addition to our own. Is there then, in our God faith and in the light it throws on evil anything of wisdom, solace, and courage which shall enable them and us the better to endure our destiny?

This much at least is gained—insight. There are occasions when anguish is so fresh and so acute that it swallows up everything except the consciousness of itself. For these hours, there is perhaps no remedy at the disposal of human wisdom. But, in the main, reason either continues to function or speedily reasserts itself. Then understanding can be a great strength, provided that it is the understanding not only of the *how* but of the *why*. Men can bear up under agony, they can even elect to undergo it if they feel that some purpose is served. What they find more intolerable than pain itself is pain that is pointless.

But, given the religious assurance, men perceive why and to what end they suffer. What wounds them in body and spirit is the past of the world still clinging tenaciously to its present. Meantime they are participants, even if in the smallest degree, in God's travail as He gives birth to a new order, not only of things, but of being. So the ordeal is invested with meaning, a meaning that is not merely personal, but universally human, and not only human, but cosmic.

Understanding their role, men can perceive their duty also. It is in the direction of reason, freedom, creativity, and compassion that God is moving through them. In the attainment of His goals lies therefore their obligation, and *sub specie aeternitatis* their function. This commitment to truth, freedom, and mercy is, to the religiously minded, of vastly larger significance than it can possibly be to those who arrive at it out of purely secular considerations. To the eye of faith, these objectives are no matter of private preference, nor even of reasoned conviction. They constitute a program written into the scheme of things, a design for man implicit in the ultimate God before man had yet come into being.

A confident hope, an assurance of a final victory over evil, are the last consequences of the God faith to those who hold it fast. In the heart of the agnostic or atheist there lurks forever a haunting, grisly fear: since all is chance, our ideals too are chance. The same fortuity which called them into existence may wipe them away. In the end the whole contest may end in a stalemate, or wrong may even emerge triumphant. Not so with the believer. He does not fight alone, or in human company only, nor with his heart torn by doubts over the outcome. Behind him, beside him and before, works that Power that drives the universe, which is also a Power that makes for righteousness. So much, then, can religious faith achieve against the experience of evil. It can open our eyes until, like Elisha's lad, we see "the chariots of fire" which hitherto were invisible to us; it can cause us to hear the cheering, emboldening words:

"Fear not, for they that are with us are more than they that are with them."

CHAPTER 2

THE SOCIAL CRISIS AND
THE RETREAT OF GOD

⚜⚜⚜⚜⚜⚜⚜⚜⚜⚜⚜⚜⚜⚜⚜⚜⚜⚜⚜⚜⚜⚜⚜⚜

FROM the folklore of northwestern Europe there has descended to us a weird and haunting myth which foretells that the day will come when the giants of chaos will rise against the gods and destroy them. Then there will be inaugurated the age, named Ragnarok by the Norse, and Götterdämmerung by the Germans—the twilight of the gods. With it, the legend continues as though in afterthought, the sun will set on man. An eternity will ensue during which the world, untenanted by deity and humanity alike, will endure in dark, formless void.

It is not often that any prophecy is fulfilled. And yet, this particular prognostication, which is little more than an imaginative excursion into the unknown on the part of primitive men, has, by some tragic chance, met with at least partial realization in our own time. For there is reason to wonder whether this generation may not be witnessing the twilight, not of the gods, but of God, that is to say, the beginning of the end of the God faith.

The dusk of God—if this be it—is no sudden apparition

32

which has taken mankind unawares. For four hundred years and more religion in the Western world has been in steady, sullen retreat. The historic churches have lost progressively in strength, prestige, and authority. They have been compelled to evacuate area after area of human interest—music, art, and literature; science, philosophy, and government—over which they had once presided as guiding genii. Their doctrines and moral insights have been rejected altogether by increasing numbers of men in each successive generation. Not in two thousand years have so many persons been unchurched as at present. Even among those who remain steadfast, the traditional creeds, ethical values, and rituals maintain themselves with increasing difficulty. There was a time when the believer was confirmed in his professions and practices by the universal assent of those about him, when his society was ordered with scrupulous care so as not to infringe on his religious sanctities. In our day, the man of religious convictions must stand almost alone in splendid but bleak near-isolation. His observances are forever coming into rude collision with the patterns of a world indifferent to them. And the modern mood is distinctly one of skepticism, a temper scarcely conductive to tranquillity in the religious life. The inference from all these considerations, as drawn by many competent observers, is that the historic religions and the doctrines they affirm have come at long last to the end of their course. Over the accuracy of this deduction there is room for debate. Only the future can give a full and final answer as to the fate of the God concept. What is indisputable is that it is under a shadow which is deep enough, even if it is not the prelude to a final eclipse.

But there was another term to the old Teutonic prediction. It assumed that when the gods departed into oblivion, men would follow after them. This element of the fable too seems to be in the process of fulfillment. Great evils are abroad in the world. They manifest themselves most conspicuously in the horrors of modern war. But they are present too in the conflicts—political, economic, and social—afoot within each society. And they struggle toward domination in the spirit of each thinking person. A large question suggests itself. What is the relation between the half-millennial withdrawal of religion and the vast social crisis of our generation? Is it one of coincidence? Or, on the contrary, does a causal relationship exist between the two phenomena? In brief, is man's twilight, as the ancient legend assumed, a necessary consequence of God's?

II

More, much more than is generally recognized, has been involved in the recession of religion in the modern world. On the surface all that appears is that church structures are being shaken, that systems of dogma are cracking up, that ritual patterns are decaying, that many men are no longer formally associated with the communions in which their fathers lived and died. But these developments, though of large import, constitute neither the whole story nor even its most significant element. The central, revolutionary fact is this: Nothing less than a *Weltanschauung* is disintegrating. Where once men looked at the cosmos and detected in it certain principles of its being, they are now likely to see it in an altogether different light.

The world outlook that is retreating is both the chief possession and the common property of the Western religions. To be sure, the churches have quarreled in the past, and still differ today, over the details of its formulation and the idioms in which it is to be expressed. In the most essential matter they have always agreed. There their concurrence is so complete that the basic affirmation of the various Judaisms and Christianities, ancient, medieval, and modern, can be caught in one brief proposition. They interpret the universe alike—as the manifestation of a God.

All insist together that beyond the Many and the Phenomenal stands the One, the Absolute, the Substance, the Shekinah or indwelling Presence. All discern in the rationality of nature, in the recurrent forms of its behavior, in the thought processes of man the Reason, the Idea, the *Logos* which is at the core of things. All affirm that in the movement of physical bodies, the surge of life, the volition of man, a universal Will or *Elan* has individualized itself. Man's freedom, his sensitivity to the beautiful, his aspiration after the good are, in their sight, but reflections of the moral character of the Being of all beings. The world then is to them an ordered world, not only in the sense that it behaves according to the laws of its own being, but in a deeper, perhaps more significant fashion. It is an expression of a Rational Will, of a sane, intelligible process. And as for the multiplicity of the names of Deity, and the diverse insights represented in them, all the historic communions would, in their less dogmatic moments, concede these to be aspects of a whole too large for any single concept. With the medieval Jewish mystic they would say—

> They parabled of Thee in many likenesses,
> Lo, through all their imaginings, Thou art One.

Into the knotty issue of the tenability of this idea, we shall not enter here. The question relevant to our inquiry is whether in the ebb tide of faith the landmarks of the centuries may not have been unmoored and swept away, whether in theological insights there may not reside vast implications for human conduct.

Given the religious interpretation of the universe, as it has just been described, what follows from it?

Man, in the first place, takes on heightened stature. For all his physical insignificance, for all the brevity of his days, he shares in the divine character. The rationality of God which slumbers in the stone as the automatisms of natural law, in him is free, conscious thought. The Will of God which in the beast appears as instinct, in him becomes moral purpose. The creativity of God is his determination to build and fashion in materials and ideas. Man, every man, is therefore in a sense God in miniature. By virtue of that fact he transcends infinitely in value the stuff of which he is composed. Indeed, he is of illimitable moral worth, for he is, in all actuality, but a little less than the angels.

And men, collectively, become one. On the surface of their beings, they may be mortal enemies, struggling competitively for food, air, shelter, security, and recognition. Yet they are all individualizations of the same Spirit, bound together under their divisions by Him. Their unity runs deeper and is more abiding than their diversity and mutual antagonisms—which is what the Judaeo-Christian tradition has meant by its insistent references to the brotherhood of all mankind.

Finally, the existence of the individual is, in the light of this faith, pointed toward goals. A manifestation of God, his fulfillment lies in the achievement and expression of that reason, freedom, creativity, and moral potentiality which are the qualities, at once human and divine, of his essential character. And as for the social order, its role is readily apparent. It is the function of man's collective life to make possible self-realization for every personality. Of these objectives it should be noted that they are derived not from ethical caprice or preference so as forever to be cursed with the taint of subjectivity; they are rooted in, and warranted by, the scheme of things.

Nature reputedly abhors a vacuum. When one *Weltanschauung* evaporates, another rushes in to fill the void. Like the religious outlook, that which is supplanting it exists in almost countless variations and shadings. Yet, once again, under all the diversities, it is one. The crucial point of distinction is the God-concept. Once this is rejected, the universe of necessity takes on other hues and colors. Inevitably it will seem fundamentally disordered, and that despite the phenomenon of natural law. A madman breathes, ingests, and secretes regularly. His body conforms to the normal rational pattern of all living things. Yet he is insane in that his actions are without intelligible objective and recognizable purpose. In this sense, reality to the atheist must partake of a lunatic temper. It is devoid of unity of ground, of ultimate reasonableness, of point.

From this view, as from its alternative, vast implications flow, but, as might be expected, of a radically different purport. Man, the by-product of a blind world machine, becomes a thing, one of many random creations. He is curiously fashioned, to be sure, and invested with extraordinary powers. Thanks to the strange composition of that colloidal solution which is his frame, he is capable of thought and aspiration, of the emotions of love and compassion. But his faculties are a passing freak of the universe. They are the phosphorescence of the slime. There is beauty in him, and about him an aura of vast sadness. But he is naked of that dignity and significance which invest him when he is regarded as a unique manifestation of the Reality of all realities, partaking of its nature and eternity.

The basic kinship among men is gone too. There is no longer a Spirit in which all participate, of which all are manifestations. At bottom, human beings now are merely the end products of a cosmic conveyer belt. And since their brotherhood in God is gone, their mutual competitiveness stands out the more boldly, tempered now only by those expediencies which self-interest dictates.

Nor is there abiding purpose left for either mankind or man. The human enterprise, in a universe that has a fate but no destiny, becomes a pain-wracked pilgrimage from one nowhere to another. The individual, an infinitesimal syllable in this idiot's tale, must take such comfort as he can from the chance experiences allowed him in the point-

less interval of consciousness between a mysterious dawn
and an equally mysterious dusk.

So much then of implication is involved in the two outlooks, one declining, the other ascending. In considering
them and their consequences, the thought suggests itself
that there may after all have been something of wisdom
in the words of Moses when he said:

"See, I have set before thee this day life and good, death
and evil. . . . Wherefore choose thou life that thou mayest
live."

III

A theory, to be worth its salt, ought to be susceptible of
verification in experience, actual or imagined. The person
who posits it should be able to say, "This is the hypothesis
I am adopting. If it be valid, I shall find such and such
in the world."

Now if we are correct in our assertion that two *Weltanschauungen* struggle against each other for mastery over
the soul of modern man and that one has for some time
been gaining the upper hand over the other, we should
be able to detect the consequences in life about us. The
temper and morality which we have described as attending
the religious outlook should be on the wane; antithetical
moods and behaviors which flow from the opposite view
should be in the ascendant. We should expect to find that
a sense of high point and purposefulness in life shall have
been succeeded by a spirit of despair and futility. Men
should furthermore have lost in reverence and gained in
contempt for the human personality. The ethic of the ultimate unity of all individualities should have yielded place

to a code according to which competition is the supreme rule. This latter morality should have become increasingly articulate with time; as the outlook on which it is based diffused itself, as its implications were more clearly perceived, and as its advocates gained in boldness—the whole process ending in an open frontal assault on the Judaeo-Christian system of values. These are the consequences we might expect to find. And it is just these which we do find.

Despite the impressive achievements of mankind, all of which should have added up to vastly heightened self-respect, it is questionable whether the human species has ever appeared so vile in its own eyes as at the present moment. In the fading glow of his Christianity Immanuel Kant could regard the heavens above and the moral law within and still feel his heart fill with increasing awe and wonder. But man today, peering through a drabber light, looks out at the vastness of time and space only to turn away chilled with a sense of insignificance. And when he directs his gaze inward, he discerns not a soul but a biochemical process. A film of sentiency on a planetary speck of dust, lost in the wildernesses of galaxies. what is there in his role or constitution to redeem his opinion of himself? That he is strongly tempted to despise himself is widely attested in contemporary literature. Joseph Wood Krutch, for example, in his *The Modern Temper,* sees the adverse influence of this self-depreciation in all aspects of contemporary thought, including even the drama.

"A Tragedy, Divine or otherwise," he asserts, "must have a hero and from the universe as we see it both the

Glory of God and the Glory of Man have departed. . . . We can no longer tell tales of the fall of noble men because we do not believe that noble men exist. The best that we can achieve is pathos and the most that we can do is to feel sorry for ourselves. Man has put off his royal robes and it is only in sceptered pomp that tragedy can come sweeping by."

Equally representative of the mood which has distilled itself from the newer world outlook is a widespread sense of frustration. In a world in which nothing means anything, the career of mankind and of the individual man cannot be regarded as particularly meaningful. It is this painful realization which motivates, among many other books of our generation, *A Preface to Morals* by Walter Lippmann. "When such men (that is, those who have abandoned the traditional religions) put their feelings into words they are likely to say that, having lost their faith, they have lost the certainty that their lives are significant." "He (the modern man) may be very busy with many things but he discovers one day that he is no longer sure they are worth doing. . . . He is possessed by a great deal of excitement amidst which, as Mr. Santayana once remarked, he redoubles his effort when he has forgotten his aim."

Insignificance and futility are, as we anticipated, the shadows which have crept over the soul of man as the old light waned. For the immediate present, there is some abatement in their intensity. Threatened by more ponderable evils, men have been compelled to concentrate their energies on the urgent task of resistance. A sense of purpose has reasserted itself, even among those who lacked it until recently. But it is a phenomenon born of the emergency of the hour, and hence necessarily transient. Should the perils pass, the psychic reaction to them will disappear also. In calmer, less dangerous days the malaises of the modern spirit will return to their normal endemic virulence.

Our other expectation has been fulfilled too, in that one moral system has among millions of men been supplanted by another. Timidly, cautiously, during recent centuries, one voice after another was raised to challenge the ethical values of the Judaeo-Christian tradition. Now in our own day the dissenters have become legion, the chorus of their denials thunders in our ears, and the walls of our social structure waver in the tumult.

The individual, it is asserted with an explicitness and a boldness unmatched in two millennia, is not by nature endowed with infinite worth, nor entitled inherently to freedom. He is but a thing to be used, a tool whereby the strong man, the state, the social revolution are to fulfill themselves. The relationship between persons is not one of co-operation. Struggle is the law of life, among men and nations alike. Not insight, understanding, or persuasion are the proper instruments for the adjustment of disputes, but coercion, naked and unashamed. And as for that mercy and compassion of which Hebrew prophets and Christian saints made so much—these are no more than a womanish and corrupting slave morality. Let the strong then prevail by virtue of their strength, and as for the weak—*vae victis*.

Among other things, an explanation, at least in part, is now available for the most paradoxical development of the modern world—that it should find itself in a state of crisis just at a time when the historic causes of crisis are at their lowest ebb. For it is out of poverty, hunger, and physical need, out of disease and frustration, out of ignorance and prejudice, that wars have flared among nations in the past, and tensions grown high within peoples. With justification then, men assumed that the measure of peace, international and social, would increase as want was diminished, as pain of the body and mind was alleviated, as superstition and group bias were mitigated by education and communication. Now all these things have in no slight measure come to pass. There is less today among men of elemental social evil than ever before. And the result? Two world conflagrations in one generation and a class struggle unequaled in history for its ferocity and destructiveness. How shall one account for this failure of all reasonable expectations? In part, the answer lies in the fact that the remedies themselves have precipitated new maladies. Thus the machine which forced back the frontiers of privation has evoked the problems of the distribution of the goods it creates. The literacy which has reduced ignorance has encouraged men to discern more clearly than ever before their legitimate claim on society and to demand its fulfillment. The instruments of communication which have brought groups closer has also increased their range of aggression against one another. And yet none of these altogether explains the fantastic contradiction of a body politic which becomes the more grievously ill, the healthier it ought to be.

The inference forces itself on us that vital elements have been progressively withdrawn from society at the very time that medicaments for its healing were being applied. Or to put it more accurately, it is not only that one of the roots of social well-being has been dying, but also that another, evil in character, has been growing cancerously in its stead. And now despite all the patient husbandry of recent generations, the whole plant is aflower with lethal blossoms and a poisonous fruitage.

IV

Weltanschauungen may work in wondrous ways their influences to exert. They may affect behavior deviously, subtly, almost imperceptibly. Again they may operate so slowly that their implications for action will be tardy in asserting themselves. From these circumstances arises the common impression that theories of the cosmos are no more than the playthings of academicians. Since this notion is widespread, it becomes necessary to expose the error implicit within it, to exhibit more closely and in greater detail how the religious and irreligious views alternatively serve as determinants of behavior.

It should be observed in passing that neither of the movements which have so profoundly molded the modern world has made the mistake of underestimating the role of ideology. Communism and fascism alike, the former more consistently, though not more resolutely than the latter, have laid heavy stress on doctrines which superficially seem far removed from their social programs. For they have recognized what the teachers of Judaism and Christianity have long known—that as a man thinks of ultimates, so he tends to deal with immediates. Or as Chesterton put it somewhere: the most relevant inquiry which a housewife can address to a prospective lodger is concerning his theology.

This is not to say that a philosophy will translate itself directly into a morality. Men may fail for a time to perceive the pragmatic corollaries of their faith; they may be aware of them but resist accepting or applying them should they be difficult of execution or repugnant morally and esthetically. But, like murder, doctrine will out.

Theism and atheism must in the long run affect human behavior materially:

first,   because a man's actions will necessarily reflect his opinion of himself;

second, because his treatment of his fellows will inescapably be influenced by his evaluation of them;

third,   the whole scheme of his conduct will inevitably respond to his interpretation of the scene in which he finds himself.

Whether then a person believes himself and all men to be gods in miniature, executing a cosmic design, or on the contrary, flotsam and jetsam floating on aimless planetary currents, is, in terms of practical implications, a matter of no slight consequence.

Again, the moral enterprise of man consists essentially of two simultaneous efforts: the quest after personal realization and the readiness to negate one's self for the sake of the collective welfare of men. But self-fulfillment and self-sacrifice are both painful, laborious activities, which therefore have to be justified in reason. In other words, a man must think well of himself and of his significance, well of the human species and its significance, or else effort on their behalf will appear to yield too little of a *quid* for the *quo;* the game will not seem deserving of the candle. It is just on these delicate but vital points that the weight of an outlook may prove decisive. Given the religious position, the individual and mankind are in the light of their nature and destiny worth a struggle. Given the antithetical attitude and haunting doubts arise that will not down. What is the sense of a painstaking program of self-negation on behalf of a humanity which is *sub specie aeternitatis* only a larger accident than the individual himself?

Last of all, men require, for joy of spirit and creativity of action, a conviction of purpose. If they cannot find it in the destiny of mankind as a whole, they will seize upon some commitment and set that up as their final goal. Just as a person who is bored with his existence may out of sheer ennui attach himself to a jigsaw puzzle or detective story and work at them as though nothing in all the world mattered so much; just as that person will be the more likely to have recourse to such flights from reality the less significance he can find in the normal processes of his life, and will concentrate the more fiercely on them, the bleaker his prospects appear to him; so with the deeper, broader business of living.

In a nontheistic, and hence nonsane universe, there can be for the human enterprise no objectives which proceed from the nature of things. Each man perforce must fix his own goals, conscious that they are subjective and even arbitrary. Fix them up he will; he cannot live without them. But then he is likely to cling to them frenziedly for they are all that stand between him and a desperate pointlessness. His aims will be neither more valid nor less valid than those of his fellows. What is more, they will tend to be partial and limited, since any ideal that embraces mankind in its entirety is too likely to raise the painful issues of ultimate significance. They may then take the relatively innocent form of art, science, or literature, not for mankind's sake, but for their own, or the much more dangerous shape of an exaggerated nationalism or class consciousness. If Mr. Aldous Huxley is to be believed, it is just these influences which are responsible for much of the passion exhibited by the Nazis and Communists over their respective programs. When the cosmos sanctions no universal purposes, men will select single, fragmentary interests, and to these they will cling with a fury all the more intense because the alternative to them is total aimlessness, and that way madness lies.

It is apparent then, despite any popular impression to the contrary, that world outlooks have, so far as influence on action is concerned, something of the character of the traditional mills of the gods. They may grind slowly but they grind exceedingly small. A belief or a disbelief cannot be locked in the skull. Sooner or later, it will escape confinement and, in one fashion or another, redirect the movements of the body and the hand.

V

Observe the word *later*. Much is contained within it. Under an innocuous surface it conceals the elucidation of some of the obscurities still remaining in our position. Among other things it resolves a paradox of which the reader has no doubt been mindful and which must have seemed to him to offer incarnate and tangible refutation of our entire thesis. We refer to that human contradiction in terms who, in view of our argument, should not exist at all: the humane, self-sacrificing atheist, the man who has rejected the Judaeo-Christian theology root and branch and yet, against all our theorizing, lives an exemplary moral life nonetheless.

Now no personality is intelligible in terms of the present only. To comprehend the living rebuttal of our case (we shall name him John Jones for sweet convenience sake) we must understand not only him but his father James as well.

James Jones, two generations removed, was like most of his contemporaries an orthodox Christian who took most seriously the doctrines and ethical principles of his church. When his son John approached the age of discretion, James charged him as follows:

"John, my boy," said he, "you will soon be responsible for your own actions. One rule I would give you—the chief commandment 'thou shalt love thy neighbor as thy self.'"

"But, Father," John queried, "why shall I love my neighbor as myself? It may not be to my interest. Besides my neighbor may be a most obnoxious fellow, or he may be my competitor, standing in the way of my ambitions."

Pat from James's tongue it all came tripping, the entire Christian rationale of the Christian morality.

"Because your neighbor is an incarnation of God and hence deserving of all the love and reverence you can muster for him; because underneath your conflicts with him, both you and he are kindred manifestations of the divine spirit; because it is to this end that you were created, to exhibit God's character and to help achieve His Kingdom. Besides

48

it is so written in the Bible which is the revelation of God's will to man."

Overwhelmed by so impressive a response, John allowed himself to be persuaded. But then he went on to college, was exposed to philosophy and the sciences, and eventually did a thorough job of rejecting the religious attitudes which his father had transmitted. He abolished God altogether. That revolutionary decision in which he has persisted ever since has made apparently little difference in his life. Reared in a Christian household, he continues to live the Christian morality, though he would not admit to its Christian character, and though, furthermore, he is no longer clear as to why he should conduct himself as he does. He is, in brief, the humane atheist who strives after the Christian virtues after he has rejected the Christian theology on which they are based, in which, indeed, they had their historic origins.

But a day of judgment may be at hand. He may find himself involved in some vast social crisis, so that adherence to his ideals will require of him large sacrifices. Then he will be compelled to search for some logic to justify that ethic which he has followed heretofore as a matter of course. On what grounds, in that hour, will be commend his morality to himself? Certainly not on those presented by his father; he does not have his father's faith. Personal expediency? But that is just the point: the ethical act, alas, is often inexpedient. Shall he invoke the threat of the policeman? But guardians of justice cannot always be relied on to be about when their presence would be most salutary, and besides it would be a sorry life which would rise no higher than the requirements of the law. Shall he urge the welfare of society? But what from his point of view is society that he should regard it, or its progress that he should take account of it? Or shall he become commonsensical and argue that if he refuses to do his bit for the traditional code, others will follow his precedent, the collective life of mankind will disintegrate, and everyone, himself included, will be out in the cold. But John is no fool. He knows full well that the run of men will continue to conform to accepted patterns of behavior no matter how he comports himself, and that if society is to fail, it will in all likelihood take so long a time in the process that he will be safely out of the world when the storm breaks. Or shall he trust his instincts, his habitual responses? Shall he tell himself that he is so constituted that only if he pursues his wonted path can he have peace of mind, that to travel any other way would outrage his conscience and strip him of self-respect? But he is well aware that his habits are the result of early indoctrination, and his conscience the residue of parental admonitions and social conditioning. And it is just these— his father's values and society's expectations which he is re-examining.

Now despite all this he may persist in being a good person. He may give of himself heroically and unselfishly. Men are often better than their philosophies. But his virtue will represent no more than a blind loyalty. It will be illogical, unjustified by reason. And a moral system which has no sanctions in thought is dangerously suspended in space. Finally, what shall John say to his son Thomas when between them there arises the question which each generation puts in turn—Why?

Like all parables, this of the Joneses is an immense over-simplification of the realities. In actuality, men are more likely to decide on ethical issues out of habit than out of a clear awareness of the issues involved in them. They are in the main determined in their behavior by indoctrination and the precedent of their fellows, by the general environmental climate in which they move rather than by intellectual analysis or moral principles. They act not out of personal reasoning but out of social conditioning.

Our account of the Joneses, therefore, requires correction. They must be multiplied by the millions living and dead who affect their behavior, and stripped of much of the intellectual sophistication and critical acumen with which we have invested them. Yet, in essence, our description of what befell them remains true to the facts. In the end the evaporation of a theology must lead to the disintegration of the morality which it feeds.

The saga of the Joneses renders intelligible the humane atheist who turns out upon scrutiny to be, not a living rebuttal of our case, but a vivid illustration of its working. It accounts for much more. It explains that moral tractability which is so characteristic of our age. So long as men are firm in their viewpoint, they will be firm in their actions, When they are unsure of their footing, they will be hesitant and indecisive in their gestures. Our original James might in actuality have despised his neighbor. But he could neither admit that fact to himself, nor exhibit it too clearly. Immovable convictions prevented. Certainly he could never consciously identify himself nor make peace with any social tendency predicated on hatred—at least not unless that movement concealed its character or provided some rationalization of itself to make it seem compatible with his commitments. But Thomas, our younger contemporary, although he will in all likelihood, thanks to parental precedent, approve of love among men, will not be too confident of the ground on which his position rests. Out of intellectual indecision he may be viable on the issue. He may retain his general attitude but allow for some exceptions to it. He may, in other words, continue to try to love all men except those he hates. Or he may acquiesce to the legitimacy for others of purposes which run counter to his own tendencies and may in the end enter into dealings with them.

About the Victorians of James's generation there was in ultimate a moral intransigeance. They deluded themselves, to be sure; they threw the robes of hypocritical virtue about their immoralities. But they could not recognize something as sin and, with untroubled conscience, engage in traffic with it. And it was always possible to strip off the veils, expose the reality behind them, and extort an admission of guilt. But Thomas, though he will have his ethical preferences, will be quite tentative about them. If sin be powerful, he will be drawn to talk terms with it. When he is confronted with ugly realities, he will be strongly tempted to accommodate himself to them. He will not be so convinced of his right and their wrong as to be incapable of getting along with them.

Our account of the Joneses reveals, last of all, why, although the retreat of religion began over four centuries ago, its cumulative effects are being felt only now. Moralities, it has been made clear, hang on long after their bases in reason are gone. Time is required for men to draw and apply the implications of shifts in outlook, for the social climate to change, for one set of standards of behavior and expectation to yield to another.

When wreckers pass through the foundations of a building, destroying here a prop and there a stay, the superstructure may remain intact for some while. It may hold together by the interweaving of boards and plaster, or in response to secondary repairs. During this period, it may continue to give every appearance of solidity. But whether through sudden strain, or slow settling, the entire fabric will either sag or crash in the end. So, for half a millennium, corrosives, intellectual and social, have been eating away at the God faith. The edifice which rested on it gave, for ever so long, no sigh of instability. But the stresses to which the fabric was subjected have grown progressively heavier, the supporting piers ever weaker. Now, at long last and belatedly, ominous cracks appear in the walls, the floors tilt crazily, gaping holes break the ceiling. The whole structure threatens to disintegrate, destroying in its collapse not only itself, but the mankind which erected it and tenanted it ever since the beginning of the human adventure.

VI

No complicated phenomenon is explicable in terms of one cause. The present situation of society, which is anything but simple, is transparently the consequence of many factors —political, economic, cultural, and psychological. Our thesis is not that the twilight of God, of and by itself, accounts for the darkness which has settled on the world. We

contend only that the retreat of religion has been a con-
tributant to the tragedy of our time, and that of the highest
order and deepest influence.

Now to demonstrate the utility of the God faith is, by
no means, to prove that God exists. My point for the present
is only that a causal relation exists between belief and behavior. Once this is perceived, inferences of large significance follow inescapably. It becomes apparent that no person of social conscience can afford to ignore religion or
dismiss it lightly—all on the erroneous assumption that
it represents merely the stock in trade of the modern witch
doctor or the moldy heirloom of intellectual obscurantists.
Theological insights are revealed in their true and vital relevance to human welfare. And it is obvious too that, in dealing with the crucial issues of our generation, we shall have
to do more than remake political structures, recast economic
processes, and reorder educational procedures, indispensable
as these tasks may be. For our world will never know peace,
internal and international, until men have reacquired faith
in life's significance, have learned to respect the human
personality, to elect the rule of co-operation, to pursue the
morality of insight, and to find their fulfillment in the
achievement of the good life for all. Without such a temper,
any social reconstruction can be little more than a rearrange-
ment into a new pattern of old, faulty materials—a method
scarcely conducive to building for the times, let alone for
eternity. But the ethical attitudes which men require for
their salvation cannot be had on order. One must first make
certain affirmations concerning life; hence concerning the

universe of which it is a manifestation; therefore, ultimately, concerning God.

This is what I have been contending all through this long involved piece of argumentation. Yet it has all been said before us in one simple formula, in that book in which very many things have been put so wisely and so well that men ever afterward have been compelled to plagiarism—

> Except the Lord build the house,
> They labor in vain who build it.

CHAPTER 3

A PROTEST AGAINST A NEW CULT

❋❋❋❋❋❋❋❋❋❋❋❋❋❋❋❋❋❋❋❋❋❋❋❋❋❋❋❋❋

THE CONVERSION of liberal churches into "Newer schools for Social Research" constitutes a modern religious revolution of the first magnitude. It has dethroned the God of the theologian and mystic and set in His place the demon of Social Justice. In the emancipated pulpit and pew there is now no God but Human Progress, the Reformer is his Prophet, and the Tables of economic statistics are his Bible.

So quiet and imperceptible have been the encroachments of this new born faith, this cult of Social Justice, that even the faithful did not sense its catastrophic character. Progressive churches have ceased to be concerned primarily with dogma and sacrament and have devoted themselves to the correction and amelioration of the injustices of our economy. A generation ago, preachers edified their congregations with discussions of the necessity of total immersion, the importance of salvation, the merits and demerits of higher criticism and, in the Jewish pulpit, the need for ritualistic reform. The congregation of our day is educated in the implications of Christianity for factory conditions, the relationship between God and trade unions, and the attitude of religion toward the problem of a more equitable distribution of the world's goods.

That a new reformation is in progress is patent. That it was born unheralded and unperceived is due to a combination of two factors. In the first place, our contemporary Luthers have been the priests of the older faiths and have remained nominally within their sectarian walls. In the second place, the transformation in religious tone and content has been affected not by a direct break with the past but by a shift of emphasis. The pianissimi of the religion of our fathers have become our fortissimi, so that, while repeating the older notes, our churches play in effect a new symphony. A transference of emphasis is often deceptive. It leads one to an illusion of continuity, even as heat passes continuously into light. But if of sufficient force, it is tantamount to a new creation. After all, light is *not* heat.

That the religion of contemporary churches is a different thing from that of a generation ago is so clear that all who run may read, if they but will. Our pulpits, at least liberal pulpits, are humanistic rather than theological. The name of God is still invoked in them. But to the socially minded preacher, that name connotes not so much the Creator or the Cosmic Soul as a sanction for ethics or an apotheosis of social ideals. The otherworldliness of traditional Christianity and Judaism has been supplanted by a very definite this-worldliness. No more vivid illustration of this fact can be found than the evolution of the doctrine of the Kingdom of God. This concept, by origin expressive in Christian and Rabbinic thought of the coming of the Messiah, the End

57

of Days, and the Resurrection, has come to represent the ideal terminal point of all lines of progress—economic, hygienic, cultural, and sociological. The Kingdom comes no more in the footprints of a mystic Anointed One but with the attainment of unemployment insurance, old age pensions, and legislation on yellow-dog-contracts. The lips still speak of salvation from sin and the grasp of death but the heart is concerned with economic redemption.

Concomitant with this inversion of stress has gone an increasing impatience with dogma and ritual. If the goal of the church is essentially the application of ethical concepts to society, any concern with doctrine and cultus must necessarily be an unwelcome distraction of attention. The new preacher is strangely disinterested in theology and rite. Never before in the history of the great Western religions have the clarity of doctrine and its exposition been as befogged as they are today. To be sure, all this has led to a breadth of mutual tolerance that is most refreshing after the din and strife of contentious creeds. But one tends to suspect that much of interchurch affection and embracing reveals not a growth of heart but an atrophy of head, that it is the interpenetration and mutual assimilation of two viscous organisms that have lost their vertebrae. Tolerance is such an honorific word; we suffer from an unfortunate temptation to admire it even when it springs from a lack of intellectual backbone.

II

The evolution of liberal pulpits into economic rostra represents the logical consequence of definite social and psychological causes. It renders vocal those protests which intelligent men have long suppressed against the stupidities, iniquities, and inadequacies of established, organized churches. It is a revulsion against all the unfortunate theological offspring of that casuistic dispute in Nicea as to the relation of the Son to the Father. It is a movement of hostile reaction to the Talmudic debate between the Schools of Hillel and Shammai as to the edibility of an egg laid on a Holyday which follows a Sabbath. It is a denial of the necessity or relevance of hypertrophied dogmatisms, sacramentalisms, and ritualisms.

But this business of substituting society for God as an object of worship and as the goal of religious activity is more than a negation of certain objectionable characteristics of Western religion. It is also a perfectly intelligible manifestation of the *Zeitgeist*, the tenor, tone, and spirit of our age. Whatever else may be said of established religions, their theologies are expressions of the rationalistic spirit. One may quarrel with their logic, their consistency, and the premises from which they spring. But, at least, they represent attempts to render reasonable the intellectual substructure of organized churches. Whether undue emphasis has been laid upon intellectualism in the historic churches is a moot point. What is certain is that the churches, through their theologians, have thrown in their lot with rationalism. And, just at present, the cause of reason happens to be an unpopular one. For now the fell spirits of antiintellectualism are abroad. The recent popularity of Bergson's intuitionism, the ascendance of William James over Josiah Royce, the dominance of Dewey—all alike are circumstantial evidence

59

of the fact that the tenor of our age is pragmatic rather than rationalistic. And the clergyman, who discovers himself clothed in the outmoded garments of Reason in an age when Social Action is all the rage, tends naturally to cast off his old cloak, without undue consideration for its possible usefulness or desirability. Even churchmen must follow the fashion.

But the tale of the rise of our new cult of social justice is not told merely by enumerating the revulsions against medieval dogmatism, sacramentalism, and rationalism. Other factors have contributed powerfully to its emergence. Not least among these must be mentioned the fact that the deification of social progress offers a most welcome refuge to the theologically disturbed. Even in these days of Eddington, Jeans, and Whitehead, the maintainance and exposition of a theology is an arduous task. Medical science has as yet discovered no way of vaccinating clergymen against the virus of new and disturbing ideas. And when philosophy and science create epidemics of doubt and uncertainty in religious issues, the minister is by no means immune. A clergyman with doubts is a very uncomfortable person. Need there be any surprise if he prefers to forget his theology and ritual which cause him his painful moments and takes refuge in the advocacy of quite unimpeachable economic reforms? Need there be any wonder if the preaching of social justice becomes the more vehement as doctrinal belief becomes the less certain? Need one marvel if the churchman who can no longer wholeheartedly assert his faith in the Fatherhood of God cries from the housetops his hope for the Brotherhood of Man?

But more potent than all of these factors is one other—
a recognition of the sterility of organized religion, its in-
efficacy and impotence in effecting its program. For two
millennia the teachers of Christianity and Judaism have
protested that in their ethic and doctrine they possessed the
alchemist's stone which would transmute human character and transform society. After twenty centuries of experiment, men are taking stock of the accomplishments
and achievements of their churches, and the balance sheet
reveals an appalling bankruptcy. Of all the pretentious
prospectus, not one clause has been converted to fact. For
all practical purposes, all the catechisms and sermons on
ethics and character might have been addressed to the
sticks and stones. Human nature has intractably refused
to be affected to any appreciable extent by beautiful texts,
even when expounded with brilliant ingenuity.

This failure to effect a program for the individual shrinks
into insignificance beside bankruptcy in an attempt to mold
the social order. The church has always insisted that it
carried a message of supreme importance for human society.
It promised to abolish war, establish the equality of all men,
prohibit exploitation of human beings, and transform the
City of Man into the City of God. Despite the collective
efforts of all cults and creeds, the sword is still a sword, not
a plowshare; the laborer is still not worthy of his hire; the
poor and the needy are even now discouragingly with us;
man lives not to serve God but the Mammon of great
corporations; and the City of Man stubbornly persists as
a hopelessly human institution, quite undisturbed by influences of the divine.

Unfortunately, the church must now answer not only for passivity and ineffectuality but even more seriously, for definite malfeasance and wrong. It is not enough that it has failed in its objectives, it has positively, actively and maliciously resisted their realization. Pledged by lip allegiance to God, the church has historically been a most resourceful ally of the Devil. The cause of sweetness and light, of liberty and happiness has had no enemy so resourceful and stubborn as the clergy of all countries and faiths. It is astounding to consider how often the church has been on the wrong side of the fence. It stood with medieval feudalism against the rising bourgeoisie; with Prussian autocracy against social democracy; with Russian tsarism against popular discontent; with rugged individualism against a planned, rationalized, co-operative economy. In the South, it was the great bulwark of human slavery; in Central and South America, the stronghold of Spanish feudalism. It has sanctioned war, blessed cannons and enthusiastically preached hate. It has resisted the liberation of woman, the liberalization of standards of domestic relations, the assertion of the will to fuller lives by submerged classes everywhere. Had its intentions been deliberate, it could not have furnished fuller support to the indictment of Marx and Engel that religion serves as the opiate of the masses. All this is asserted in full recognition of glorious exceptions to the unhappy rule, with full awareness of the rebels who inherited the mantle of the prophets. The fact is irrefutable—the church has been one of man's greatest obstacles in his social progress.

And now, churchmen who are not blind have come to

decipher the handwriting on the wall. The same history which has given the freethinker his most damaging ammunition has given the clergyman and his laity a melancholy sense of futility and defeat. Pulpit and pew are awake to vulgar gossip concerning social skeletons in ecclesiastical closets. They know that they are being weighed in the balance, that their claims and pretensions are being measured against actual accomplishments. They recognize that they have been found wanting.

Liberal clergymen realize that judgment cannot long be deferred, that the next generation of ecclesiastical polity must render atonement for the sins of twenty centuries. An awareness of the necessity of immediate action, a sense of now or never, have called forth the tone of nervous urgency and half-hysterical determination with which the new pulpit preaches its doctrine. A terror haunts the minister who is conscious of rising tides, the fear that what happened in the first French Republic and Soviet Russia may be repeated in America—or even worse—a dread lest the church rot away in the silence of its own ineptitude, discarded by society in its evolution as so much worthless impediments. Hence the resolution that when the *Dies Irae* dawns, the church will stand, clear and vindicated, on the side of the angels.

This, then, is the sociological recipe of the new cult that has been born to us: Take one part of protest against the relevance of theological casuistry, one part of revulsion against the necessity of cancerous ritualisms, one of the pragmatic and socially centered tone of the times; compound with seven parts of a recognition of the passive failures and active iniquities of the church in society and, then, as from some witch's caldron, boils forth an elixir to rejuvenate and transform organized religion.

III

At this point, a vigorous disclaimer must be entered, a categorical denial made. It is not my purpose to render aid and comfort to the dogmatic medievalist, the hair-chopping ritualist, the obscurantist, or the social reactionary. I will not make common cause with the backwoods exhorter, the worshipers of theological yesterdays, and the advocates within the church of the economic and social status quo. I have little patience, for that matter, with the attitude that the church keep hands off every serious issue that confronts mankind. I am keenly aware of the fact that the social message of religion has unfortunately been played down to the point of disappearance, that the church has failed in its mission to society. I, too, dread a righteous judgment. I am cognizant of the urgency and necessity that impel the teachers of the new cult. As a matter of fact, I go with them a long way—but at one point I stop short. I will not be stampeded by the liberal rush to make of religion a lopsided matter of procuring certain bills from legislatures. To such legislation I may give sincere approval, but I insist that there is more to religion than social justice, important as that may be.

Mine is a plea for equilibrium and balance. For religion is a complex affair, answering to a multiplicity of needs of which the direction of human relationships is only one among several. The church, especially the liberal church, stands today in imminent danger of sanctioning a cannibalism in which one aspect of its being threatens to absorb the whole. An emphatic word of warning is certainly in order.

IV

Now, if my plea for balance in religion is to be both cogent and intelligible, it is necessary, at this point, to consider at least some of the multiple manifestations of the religious life, to analyze into its discrete parts that organic whole which is the church. Only such a dissection will reveal the abiding value of those elements which the new cult threatens to submerge.

A most superficial survey of the historic nature of religions will reveal how far they transcend in their interests the cause of social justice. For churches exist in response to four distinct and diverse human needs, four fundamental hungers and aching voids in human life, and only when all of these four have been satisfactorily answered can any organized religion claim a faithful discharge of its duties. Man approaches his priest with a fourfold need—the church dare not dismiss him satisfied in only one. The gift of water is not sufficient for one who asks for food, clothing, and shelter also.

A complete church, therefore, one which makes competent answer to life's challenge, must comprise in its program and scope at least the following four aspects.

1. *A ritual*

The most deliberately lean and ascetic church finds outward expression in fixed forms of worship, collective activities and prearranged patterns of group conduct, in brief, in a body of ritual, a cultus. For an organized religion represents an attempt to assert in unison theological affirmations, ethical attitudes, and emotional intuitions. A ritual serves then as the etiquette of the social life of a religion.

In most primitive religions, the ritual so completely overshadows all other phases of the religious life that sociologists like Durkheim, who approach religion via anthropology, tend to define religions exclusively as forms of group conduct. Changes in taste, together with periodic iconoclastic outbreaks, have transformed the nature of these group patterns and relegated them to a comparatively secondary position. But even today, a ritual is a desirable inevitability in any church. An inevitability, because people assembled for a common purpose must do something; desirable, because a ritual affords a visible manifestation of an intellectual attitude, a stimulant of emotions and a conveyance of ethical values. Besides, there are always with every church those who are fascinated by ritualistic forms and cheered by the prospect of participation in group activity. How, otherwise, shall one account for those exotic organisms called the Fraternal Orders of Wolves, Bears or whatnot; how shall one explain the lusty chanting of our American luncheon clubs? And as to those who attend churches only to kneel, to sing hymns, or to watch processions attended by the burning of incense or the bearing of symbols, who dare say to these that religion has no bread for their peculiar hunger—naïve and ingenuous though it be?

66

2. *A focus and stimulus of the religious emotion*

No self-respecting church fails to pay tribute to the emotional life of man, especially in our day, when the "religious experience" has been ushered into its own by professors of psychology. All the external manifestations of organized religions represent carefully elaborated avenues of approach to the life of feeling. Organs, incense, stained glass, and curious vestments have all been devised to evoke intuitions of awe, reverence, elevation, peace, and blessedness. Sonorous phrases, vividly imaginative doctrines, and exotically embroidered rituals are intended to serve a dual purpose: on the one hand, to charge the intellectual and pragmatic aspects of religion with an aura of emotions; on the other hand, to harness all the tempestuous energies of spontaneous and uncultivated feelings, to focus them about the church and, thereby, to furnish colorful momentum and drive to pallid theologies and ethics.

Anticlericals have characterized this concern with the senses as deliberate pandering to the nonrational traits of human nature. The charge is grossly unfair. The cultivation of the emotional life is a legitimate concern, its enrichment an act of beneficence, and the church is entirely within its rights in deliberately fertilizing human emotion and consciously directing its powers to its own uses. No religion can be called complete that does not have some place for a gamut of emotional experiences ranging from the pale religious aestheticism of Santayana and Pater to the fiercely blinding illumination of the mystic's communion. William James and his psychopathic saints, Schleiermacher and his sense of dependence, and Rudolf Otto with his awareness of the Holy—for all these religion must find a niche. And the persistent success of the great cults reveals the fact that the churches have long revised the classic definition of man as "homo sapiens" to read "Homo et sapiens et sentiens."

3. *A philosophy—a Weltanschauung—a reasoned scheme of things*

"Teach me Thy ways," mankind demands of a silently inscrutable universe. What is this panorama that unrolls itself before man's contemplation? Is it a monstrous horror ground out by some blind chance with no more significance than a "tale told by an idiot" or is it the outward manifestation of the Phenomenology of Spirit? And man—what is his place in the whole? Is it that of some poor player fretting his brief hour out into silent futility or that of some necessary part of the whole without whom the universe in its totality cannot find completion?

These are the questions to which men demand responses from their churches and to which at all times religions have given answer. No religion is worth its salt that has no food for the intellectual hunger of men. That is why every great religion has been prolific in theologians and philosophers. Job, Philo, Augustine, Maimonides, and Aquinas—all offer testimony to the fact that it is an indispensable function of churches to furnish their communicants with a philosophy of the universe, that religions must satisfy man's demand for a knowledge of the meaning of things, that they must, either through a God idea or otherwise, give him a sense of cosmic significance.

The possibility and adequacy of cosmic schemes taught by the church, the extent to which such world pictures can be disinterestedly rational, these are just now irrelevant questions. The fact is that without a theology, a religion is a jelly. The fact is also that every great church has answered cosmic questions by a philosophy. To one who asks the why of things, a program of social reform is an astoundingly irrelevant rejoinder.

4. *A system of ethics*

Man not only thinks and feels, he is confronted, willynilly, with the necessity of acting. And he prefers to act purposely and with a sense of direction. The need for guidance, for patterns of conduct, and objectives in procedure, is one of the greatest of human wants. The satisfaction of that need has always been a function of religion. The presence of the church in moral and ethical realms has often been resented, either on grounds of selfish interest or else on theory, as an indefensible intrusion of the supernatural into purely human considerations. And yet, the moral interests of organized religions are perfectly intelligible. For the ethics of religion is an inevitable consequence of its philosophy and theology. Given a *Weltanschauung,* and a code of action flows from it logically and naturally. Churches have taught bad ethics and good ethics, but they have always taught ethics. And if man insists on instruction, the church has as much historic right to set itself up as teacher as has the state, the press, or secular schools of philosophy. The danger discerned in religion's concern with morality is not trespassing, it is an absorption of the whole by a part.

These then are the fourfold aspects, the quadruple functions of any organized sect. For purposes of analysis, we have divided them into discrete and disparate activities. The fact of the matter is that the religious life is an organic unity with a Bergsonian "interpenetration of parts," not susceptible in reality to any such dissection. As in any organism, the divergent aspects fuse and merge so completely that it is not possible to say where one begins and the other leaves off. The cultus, the emotionalism, the theology, and the ethic intertwine and melt into each other so that any use of the scalpel leads to a falsely simple intellectualistic analysis.

Nevertheless, and in despite of the organic unity of the religious life, a sect may, like any other living thing, suffer either a hypertrophy or atrophy of one of its essential parts. The history of religions offers abundant evidence of lack of balance due to unequal emphasis. The Unitarian Church and Ethical Culture, for example, afford full programs of philosophy and ethics but virtually nothing else. The religion of Royce is pure intellectualism and morality, that of James blankly sterile emotionalism. Similarly, the Judaism of the Talmud is overwhelmingly ethical and ritualistic whereas that of Philo or Maimonides, by a shift of stress, is virtually a different religion because of a predominating rationalistic trend. It is profoundly significant that no church without a full program has ever made a successful bid for popular support, that every great religion has at times experienced internal upheavals as some neglected aspect of its life boisterously reasserted itself.

V

The grounds of protest against the new cult of social justice should by now be apparent. It is not directed against the cause of reform as such nor against the attempt of the church to assert its ideals in the teeth of an unidealistic society. A religion that does not attempt to effect its moral values might just as well not have any.

And yet the church must not be stampeded into a head-long rush in one direction. Religion dare not lose its balance if it is to fulfill its function; it dare not, by a shift in emphasis, make itself entirely what it is only in part. It must not give to those who come to it with four needs, the satisfaction of only one. To those who ask for a philosophy, an enrichment of the emotional life, forms of group action as well as guidance in social life—programs of economic and political reform are not enough. All four needs are real, and men will find satisfactions for them, if not in one church, then in another; and if no church responds in full, they will perforce turn elsewhere.

There is one last issue to which the attention of our ecclesiastical pan-ethicists should be called. The danger in this business of turning churches into economic forums lies not alone in the fact that legitimate questions are left unanswered. A subtler peril is involved, a real threat that, by concentrating exclusively on social morality, the church kick the props from under its ethical system.

For in the last analysis, the ethic of the church, its

values, and ideal social patterns flow from its theology. The Brotherhood of Man is not a self-evident postulate, an axiomatic judgment. It acquires its truth only as a corollary of another concept—the Fatherhood of God. And so with the other moral values of religion; genetically and logically they derive from definite world-outlooks and theological viewpoints. The ancient prophet's insistence on his vision for mankind was not based on any ability to demonstrate the rationality of that vision. To him it was an inescapable consequence of the particular God idea he had postulated. And the church that has discarded its theology, together with the ritual and emotional experience that give it momentum and weight—the church that has turned to exclusive advocacy of a social program and ethical concepts may discover too late that it has hewed away the very foundations of its system of values, has dug a pit into which church, minister, and moral objectives shall all collapse for want of proper support.

VI

These views will, in all probability, not be greeted with a chorus of welcome. I shall be charged with deliberate sabotage of the effort to make religion socially effective, accused of applying the brakes to the moral enthusiasm of the church at a time when society needs it most. I shall be catalogued with conservatives, reactionaries, obscurantists, and other unpleasant people. Nor will I be hailed as good fellow by the clergy of the old church school; I have said too many unkind things about ecclesiastical passivity, over-absorption in theology and cult, and the failure of the churches to effect their ostensible programs. One who advocates temperance and moderation, equilibrium and balance, must expect to find himself assailed on both sides.

But when clergymen drop most of their equipment to climb onto a liberal bandwagon I, before mounting to my own place, feel that I must pick up, and attempt to restore to their owners, quite valuable bundles which have been lost in the mad scramble for seats.

All that I seek here is a balanced sense of values, a retention of precious religious paraphernalia. My sole purpose is to remind my contemporaries in organized churches of that ancient bit of Greek wisdom which distills into two words what I have been trying to say:

Meden Agan—Nothing to excess.

II

JUDAISM
AND THE AMERICAN SCENE

CHAPTER 4

THE FUTURE OF JUDAISM IN AMERICA

WHAT are the types of Jewish life which have evolved and are evolving in America and which of them is to be preferred?

Out of the past come the men and women who make up the Jewish group, their institutions, their traditions, religious and social. Over them play the alchemic reagents of American social forms, the acids and elixirs of modern ideals and ideologies. And we, transported momentarily in imagination outside the seething brew, seek to discover what is happening to American Jews, what form their group life is taking. The most superficial glance reveals that five distinctive patterns of Jewish living are being created—each possessed of colors, properties, and virtues peculiar to itself. It is the character of these which we shall explore successively. And since our description will involve critical judgments, out of it will emerge a program.

Out of the increased obstacles to assimilation on the one hand, and out of pure inertia on the other, there exists in American Israel a growing body of Jews whose Jewishness can be characterized as that of the empty vessel. Ignorant of their own past, untouched by Jewish belief, uninspired by traditional moral patterns, unassociated with Jewish institutions, indifferent to the future of Judaism, their Jewishness consists only in their feeling that they are Jews, and that other Jews and, what is more important, Gentiles, regard them as such. That such a type of Jewishness is undesirable is immediately apparent. It is a vessel without content, form without substance, a name without meaning. It can be argued with plausibility that it might be better for such Jews to be assimilated, better for them in that they would be freed from the restraints imposed on minority groups, better for Judaism in that it would be liberated from their dead weight, and better for American society from the midst of which a meaningless surface of friction would be eliminated.

The second pattern of Jewish living now evolving on the American scene is one in which the Jewish group has become a Society of Self-Protection and Mutual Aid, a magnified and glorified *Unterstützungsverein,* organized for the dual purpose of collective defense against anti-Semitism and for the care of the Jewish sick and aged, the widow and the orphan. Among American Jews there are hundreds whose Jewishness expresses itself only in philanthropy and the repelling of hostility. I have no desire to deprecate either activity. The prophets and sages too were concerned about the security of the Jews; certainly they were philanthropists. Yet it would be a tragic irony of history if this were all that were to survive from their heritage. In the lives of Jews of this type, Judaism takes on the character of a beleaguered hospital and the function of the Jew that of alternately tending the sick and manning the walls. But when the sick are well again, there is no city of habitation for them, and when the defenders are off duty, there are no shrines, homes, or libraries within the ramparts they have defended to make their defense significant.

On these two patterns of Jewish living it is relatively easy to form firm and precise judgments and to reject them for their essential negativism. It is when we turn to the two next more positive forms that we become confused and hesitant.

The third pattern of Jewish living perceptible in America is that which might well be designated as the synagogue suspended in space, the Judaism which is a religion and nothing more. There are thousands of American Jews who proceed on the assumption that the Jewish group of which they are a part constitutes exclusively a credal communion. Under this presupposition they feel that only one institution is legitimate, the synagogue, or rather the synagogue plus those organizational forms through which it expresses its ethical values. From their point of view there is but one interest which is proper and that is the interest in worship and the translation of worship into action. Such a definition of Judaism and the program which flows from it have been subjected to careful analysis. For the present it will suffice to say the theory has been rejected as inconsistent with the historic character of Judaism, as in contradiction with the actualities of the Jewish group. In practice, it has led to a Jewishness too truncated and anemic to be either meaningful or self-sustaining. Most recently the acknowledged custodians of this pattern of living have been driven to recast their theory and to strike out for a fuller program of action than was possible under it.

The fourth pattern is diametrically the opposite of the one we have just discussed. I refer to Jewish humanism, the attitude that Judaism is a culture or civilization in which religion, whatever may have been its function in the past, now possesses no place. The Jew who proceeds from such a presupposition, whether deliberately formulated or inarticulately held, lives a significant Jewish life. He possesses a sense of Jewish identity that is strengthened by his actions, he is concerned over the rights of Jews as American citizens and over Jewish philanthropies—but his program is much larger. He is interested in the Hebrew language and literature, in Jewish educational agencies and trends, in Palestine as a cultural center of world Jewry, in Jewish art, music, and belles lettres. Such a form of Jewish living puts significant content into the vessel of a Jewish identity; it reaches beyond the negativism of a Judaism which is pure philanthropy into more positive realms. Under it the Jew is enriched as an individual by Jewish culture and by his communion with it, stimulated by activities that are creative. He is, as an American citizen, the more valuable because he brings to the treasury of American spirituality the unique and divergently colored contributions of another civilization. It is meaningful, useful, stimulating, this secular culturalism—and it is not enough.

The Judaism of the vanishing synagogue, no matter how well organized it may be in communal structure, no matter how rich in art and belles lettres, is inadequate.

First, because it is not true to the historic character of Judaism.

Second, because secular culturalism is not only untrue to the historic character of Judaism but is untrue on just that aspect of Judaism which has always been at once the driving force and climactic expression of Jewish group life. In the light of our Jewish past, secular culturalism is playing Hamlet without the Melancholy Dane.

Third, secular culturalism leads immediately to embarrassments in practice. For in all its long evolution, religion has been root and flower of Jewish life and the person who wishes his Judaism without religion is likely to find it dogging him despite his preferences. For the religious aspect of Judaism has interpenetrated the whole organism, and so long as Judaism remains recognizably what it has always been, there will be no comfort in living a Jewish life unless first peace has been made with God and the God idea.

Fourth, secular culturalism is not enough because Jews too are human beings. As such they too stand face to face with the universe and seek to understand it. Like other men of all races and times they are reluctant to believe that reality is but a tale told by an idiot, a theory that is logically an incomprehensibility and practically the counsel of despair. They too grope for a *Weltanschauung* which shall at the same time clarify their insight into reality and endow their lives with meaning. They too need the assurance that their moral aspirations are, far from being mere convention and caprice, grounded in the inmost nature of things. In brief, Jews together with mankind generally need religion, need

God as a principle of explanation, as value endowing, as a sanction for morality.

And it would be an intolerable paradox if through the secularization of Jewish life Jews should be compelled to go to other cultural groups for the very spiritual satisfactions which Judaism gave to the world.

Fifth and last of all, secular culturalism is not enough because the vitality of any culturalism springs from a sense of its meaningfulness, and nothing in the universe can have abiding meaning if the universe as a whole is devoid of it. For, without a God-faith, the career of reality is but the interplay of chance and any part of reality is no more. A man may, if he choose, lose himself in some activity from a crossword puzzle to efforts on behalf of five-year plans, the deification of some social class, the glorification of some nation, the enhancement of some culture. So long as he is absorbed in his task, his very absorption gives him the sense of meaningfulness. But the moment he lifts his eyes, the universe comes within his vision and he knows at that moment, if he thinks at all, that his efforts are significant only if reality be such as to permit of significance. A religious interpretation of the universe is a prerequisite for clear-eyed enthusiasm. So it has always been in the Jewish past. So it is now.

And the culturalist, when he analyzes his position, must recognize that his zeal for Jewish culture demands a theological base; that it cannot permanently remain secular, it must become one with the fifth pattern of Jewish living emergent on the American scene—religious culturalism, the sole pattern which is true to the nature of historic

82

Judaism, adequate and self-sustaining both in theory and practice.

What is religious culturalism? It is that theory and pattern of Jewish living which takes as its basic premises the following. First, Judaism is larger in scope than religion alone. It is a culture and civilization, with all the diverse but interrelated interests and activities that make any culture. Second, religion is an integral part of Jewish culture, serving at once as the driving motif and as the climactic expression of it. And third, Jewish religion like the whole of Judaism must be traditional in character if it is to be vital and dynamic.

It is here that the Jewish Theological Seminary stands in a unique position, for it alone among analogous institutions is built on the premises of religious culturalism. The Seminary of America has always proceeded on the assumption that Judaism is a way of life. It has consistently spoken in terms of historic Judaism—terms which, for all that they are not altogether exact equivalents with it, imply a Jewish culturalism. Indeed the essential spirit of the Seminary can be caught in a restatement of an old Latin epigram, *Nihil Judaicum alienum mihi puto:* nothing which is Jewish do I regard as alien to myself. The Seminary has not only had the broadest conception of Judaism, it has insisted steadfastly on the indispensability of religion in Jewish life. Last of all, the Seminary has always been traditional in character. It has sought to reinterpret traditional Jewish values so that without sacrifice of their essence they take added relevance for the contemporary scene. The Seminary is then by its temper, its spirit, and its ideals the main instrument for the attainment of a religious culturalism. It is the institution to which American Jewry can turn with greatest confidence for the evolution of those procedures and techniques which shall translate the vision into reality. If the difficulties that lie in the way of the attainment of these goals be large, the goals are eminently worth the effort of attainment. Should we succeed in building on the American scene the type of religious culturalism which I have described, should we succeed in making this the dominant, normative type of Jewish living in this country in preference to and over and above other forms which are now emerging, then two significant objectives shall have been realized. Judaism will take on enhanced meaning and significance for the American Jew. He will find his existence endowed with all the treasures of a great cultural heritage which supplies him at the same time with meaningful religious and moral values; and, enriched and spiritualized, he will then bring into the general fund of American resources his enhanced personality and the cultural wealth of which it is possessed.

CHAPTER 5

A SPECIMEN JEW

WHEN the Christian of whatever denomination leaves the church on a Sunday morning, his religion demands of him that he shall seek to carry over into his weekaday life the theological insights, moral principles, and ritual practices which he has affirmed in public worship. Large, solemn, and difficult of execution as these requirements may be, they are virtually the sum total of his Christian obligations.

The Jew who makes his way homeward from the synagogue of a Saturday morning is expected to assume analogous duties. But with these his tasks as a Jew can scarcely be said to have begun. In the first instance, he is as a Jew associated not merely with a religious fellowship, but with cultural tradition as well. The past hands on to him an awareness, if not a knowledge, of a long history. It offers him a literature and a language, a music and an art, a system of folkways, a treasury of folklore, and a structure of institutions. He is, in brief, actually or potentially, the heir of a second complete civilization in addition to that of America with which, if he is at all typical, he has wholeheartedly identified himself. A large, vexatious issue forces itself upon him. What shall he do with this second differential heritage? Shall he accept it in toto? Shall he attempt to be an eclectic about it? Shall he be done with it all, reject it root and branch, and content himself with the quite abundant spiritual resources of America? Or shall he wash his hands of the problem and let it go by default?

This extremely difficult decision is complicated further by a number of considerations. For example, he may, as many Jews have done, take to himself the religious aspect of Judaism and refuse the cultural. Or he may, following the precedent of others, elect to do just the reverse. Again, he—or if not he, then multitudes of his fellows—is likely to be quite uninformed as to the content of the Jewish tradition. There was a time, and that not so long ago, when Jews were, by and large, extraordinarily literate in their heritage. That time is no more. So that, should our specimen Jew decide that he does wish to avail himself of the second civilization, he must, in all probability, first submit to instruction as to its character. Gravest of all, he is aware, if he is at all alert, that both the theology and culture of his fathers need some serious overhauling if they are to function effectively in his life. For four hundred years, Judaism was isolated within ghettos, untouched by the revolutions, scientific and social, afoot in the world. Only during the last century was contact re-established between it and the larger society. It is still too early for the process of adjustment to have completed itself.

But even if our specimen Jew—it should be apparent by now that he cannot be called typical, for he still frequents

the synagogue on the Sabbath and is unusual in his awareness of the problems of his being—were to be altogether
indifferent or actively hostile to the Jewish religion and
culture, he would still be called on to deal with Jewish issues.
For Jews are not only potential participants in a church and
a tradition, they constitute in all actuality a specific social
grouping. Against this identification of themselves they
may protest and theorize to their heart's content. It remains
a reality for which they may be penalized socially, from
which flight is next to impossible. Inevitably they are worried over anti-Semitism and the threat of its intensification.
Since they are Jews, Jewish philanthropic agencies will feel
free to solicit their support both on behalf of enterprises in
their own community and for the relief of distressed and
persecuted Jews abroad. It is of little consequence then that
the content of the Jewish tradition is devoid of meaning for
any particular Jew and that he might prefer not to be
marked as a Jew. He is so regarded nonetheless by the world
at large and by other Jews. Willy-nilly, he must assume
at least some of the responsibilities that flow from that fact.

But his association with the Jewish group is likely to
touch him more intimately, at the very core of his being.
For, as a Jew he is subject to certain psychic influences, of
which he may be unaware but which may affect his personality adversely nonetheless. Thus, he tends to regard
himself as not altogether wanted by the majority society of
which he wishes to be part, the approval and acceptance
of which he desires earnestly. Again, he is inclined to feel
that his Jewishness exposes him to a special set of insecurities
beyond those which are the lot of all men of his station.

What is more, he has doubtless at sometime or other had occasion to conclude that some of his frustrations, economic, social, or cultural, are the result not of personal deficiency but of the fact that he is a Jew. Last of all, as a member of an out-group, he is peculiarly sensitive and susceptible to in-group opinion. The anti-Semite when he talks about Jews rarely addresses himself to them, but Jews overhear and may quite readily be convinced that the criticisms are quite justified by the facts, and applicable, not to them of course, but to their fellows. The upshot of all this is that many an American Jew is in mortal peril of losing his sense of worth, his self-respect, his dignity in his own eyes. He may feel secretly ashamed of his Jewishness, tempted to render it inconspicuous or to conceal it altogether. He may sigh wistfully over the delights and securities of a non-Jewish identity, and wish that the lines had fallen for him in more pleasant places. He may be haunted by the misgiving that, by very virtue of the fact that he is Jewish, he is somehow a human being inferior to the Gentile. In extreme instances he will be bitter about his Jewishness, resentful of Judaism, of the Jews, and of himself because they are all tarred with the same brush.

It is an elementary principle of psychology that a person must approve of himself if he is to be happy and creative. That is not to say that he must view himself through a haze of idealizing self-approbation. On the contrary, it is desirable that he be realistic about the facts of his being and sharply critical of them. But he must, in the end, respect what he is fundamentally. Neither joyousness in living nor the will to realize one's potentialities are possible without

88

this precondition. It is this *sine qua non* of psychic health which the American Jew is in danger of losing.

Such are the problems, recognized and unperceived, which beset our specimen Jew. Over the question of how they are to be dealt with, he and his fellows differ widely and quarrel bitterly. Any Gentile who believes that all Jews stand together in a kind of monolithic unity, ought to eavesdrop when Jews discuss the issues of their being as Jews. He will be relieved of at least one misapprehension.

II

There are in the last analysis only three courses open to any Jew as he comes to grips with the problems we have described: the indifferentist, the assimilationist, and the survivalist.

The first of these can be dismissed out of hand as being less a policy than the absence of one. It consists in refusing to think systematically or act consistently about the whole business. It is, in brief, a tactic of drift intermingled with the Micawberish hope that it will all somehow come out right in the end. Obviously, it holds out no prospect of alleviating any of the vexations of Jewish living. Indeed, it suffers from all the disadvantages of both purposeful programs without the premise of either. As such, it need detain us no longer.

It is either on a survivalist "to be" or an assimilationist "not to be" that every earnest Jew must ultimately take his stand. Once one or the other is elected, secondary questions of implementation arise: how best can the Jewish group and its tradition be liquidated; how, in the event of the alternative choice, can they be preserved. But on the central fundamental issue a prior decision is in logic and practice unavoidable.

Shall the Jewish group deliberately strive to pass out of existence? For this course an impressive case can be made. It can be argued on its behalf that it will ultimately solve "the Jewish problem" by dissolving Jews. It will mean, if carried to successful completion, that the Jew will be relieved of the social burdens of a minority identity, and emancipated from the necessity of dealing with the knotty problems of adjusting his ancestral religion and second culture to their scene. A surface friction within the American community shall have been eliminated. The individual Jew will be free to dedicate all his energy and creative potentialities to the enhancement of American life, undistracted by the demands of another tradition.

I believe that I understand the assimilationist approach and appreciate whatever of cogency it possesses. Yet, I am compelled to repudiate it. In the first place, it sets a goal that is impossible of achievement. An occasional Jew may succeed in losing himself in the non-Jewish world. But most Jews are going to have to remain Jews, no matter how they may struggle against that fate, if no other reason than the pressures of the enveloping society. The largest result of assimilatory effort in the past has been to dejudaize Jews without winning for them Gentile acceptance. Nor is it likely to be more efficacious in the determinable future. The probabilities are that assimilation for Jews will be even more difficult a generation hence than a generation ago.

Paradoxical as it may seem, I who am a Jewish survivalist

am not happy over the fact that assimilation is impossible. For while I should like other Jews to choose to remain Jews in the largest and most significant sense, I resent the exercise of compulsion against them. I believe in freedom for all individuals, including the freedom of my fellows to leave my company and abandon an enterprise that means so much to me. I know that a society which will not permit Jews to quit being Jews, is also a society which by its temper will make life difficult for all Jews, regardless of their Jewish attitudes. And it has been my experience that Jews who are forced back into Judaism are often a doubtful blessing to the Jewish community. They are unwilling participants in it, indifferent to its aspirations, rebellious against its very existence. All in all, the closing of exit doors about the Jewish group is no occasion for a gleeful rubbing of hands on the part of anybody except the anti-Semite. The fact remains, however, that the assimilationist case founders on the rock of practicability.

But there is more that must be said against it. It is not calculated to do much to restore the shaken self-respect of American Jews. Quite the reverse, since its doctrine, no matter for what reason, is "cease to be what you are," its total effect is likely to be an aggravation of the sense of inferiority, already so widespread among them. Nor is the assimilationist approach altogether unexceptionable on ethical grounds. It is in no slight measure a yielding to anti-Semitism. And it is questionable whether man is ever morally justified in submitting to the intrusions of coercion.

But most of all, I reject the course of group dissolution because it represents wanton waste, the deliberate throwing away of a large cultural tradition, capable of enriching largely the individual Jew and the broader society of which he is a part. It is a solution of Jewish problems as suicide is a solution of individual problems, in a final, irretrievable expungement not only of life's difficulties, but of its opportunities as well.

III

What then is the alternative? With the blanket word, survivalist, I have covered a number of theories and programs, which concur only in that they wish to preserve some aspects of the Jewish tradition on the American scene but which differ over almost everything else: which elements are to be maintained, in what form, and how. A description and critique of all the survivalist philosophies would far outrun the limits of this paper. It would require pausing long over details. The reader will, in all likelihood, be better served should a specimen position be presented. For that purpose, I have selected the one I know best and most intimately—my own. It is not quite typical. As a rabbi, I am in a sense a Jew by profession. But there are enough Jews who are not rabbis, who live as I do, to make this the pattern representative of a large group.

What do I get out of my Jewishness—both the religion and culture (it is both to me)—to justify the expenditure of time and energy upon it? How am I the better off for my adherence to it?

From the Jewish heritage, I have derived my world outlook, a God-centered interpretation of reality in the light of which man the individual is clothed with dignity, and the career of humanity with cosmic meaning and hope; a morality, profoundly humane, elevated in its aspirations yet sensibly realistic; a system of rituals which interpenetrates my daily routines and invests them with poetry and intimations of the divine. To be sure, I have had to do some tinkering on the traditional apparatus, I have had to recast theological doctrine into consonance with the scientific picture of reality. Thus, the Biblical notion of divine creation has yielded to one that takes cognizance of the evolutionary process. In my reconstructed viewpoint God is manifest in natural law and its regularity, rather than in miracles which are a breach of it. Again I have had to do my own applying of the social values of the Jewish ethic to the political and economic issues of America. Jewish morality has always emphasized the sanctity of the individual, the social use of wealth, the principle of co-operation rather than that of coercion. But these ideals were conceived and came to maturity in a world different from and simpler than ours. Mine then has been the task of determining exactly what decision these conceptions require in moot questions such as democracy versus totalitarianism, collective bargaining and the right to strike, birth control, war and peace. The ancient sages of Israel would perhaps have been amazed by the complexity and gravity of the social situations through which I am compelled to make my way. They would, I hope, recognize the operations of their principles in the decisions I reach.

And for all my loyalties to ancestral folkways they exhibit quite clearly adaptation to the forms and exigencies of life about me. Thus, I have no scruples about the use of the radio and the phonograph on the Sabbath, even though the kindling of light and hence the release of electrical energy are forbidden by the rules of ritual law. It seems to me when I listen to the broadest of the opera or to a symphonic recording that I am, despite any technical transgression, better realizing the essential purpose of the Sabbath, which is spiritual refreshment. On the night of Passover I celebrate the exodus from Egypt in observances much like those of my forefathers. But the tale I relate is drawn from a text adapted by modern Jews from that in general use for centuries. And while the traditional account is there, much more is made of the universal significances of freedom. It is not of Israel's freedom alone that we discourse, but of all mankind, and not of political freedom merely, but economic, intellectual, and cultural as well.

Now it is quite conceivable that I might have achieved analogous results without the Jewish past. Analogous results, perhaps, but in no case, identical. For like all historic religions, Judaism has a character of its own. Its uniqueness—needless to say, this word carries no implications of superiority—consists, first of all, in differential emphases. A few illustrations selected at random may be in place to give body to this point. For example, the role of learning and study as a religious exercise, and as a key to salvation, is extraordinarily large in the Jewish tradition. Again, salvation is conceived as not an objective for the individual only but for his society as well, the former being regarded as virtually impossible without the latter. Judaism, in contrast with most Christian confessions, is relatively unconcerned with matters of creed. It is less interested that Jews shall believe alike than that they shall strive to realize the same moral objectives. But even where the accents are not different from those of other communions, the ritual expressions are. Jews, for instance, erect tabernacles to mark the season of the harvest, so contributing a special tint to the autumnal colorations of society. Last of all, the entire religious corpus is the outgrowth of a distinct cultural process. It has, because of its antecedents and associations, an individuality peculiar to itself. Any idea or value, no matter how widely diffused, is in Judaism modified by the whole tradition. The concept of Freedom for a Negro is likely to be associated with Lincoln, for all Americans with Washington, for me as an American Jew the sound of the word recalls these too, but also Moses and the Maccabees.

In brief, though I share with liberal Christians large areas of affirmation, I find myself in a special position, which simultaneously satisfies me and serves also as a foil, goad, and stimulant to other persuasions. Besides, the materials of Judaism lie at hand, ready for me to use. It would be uneconomical not to exploit them. Finally, it has been my observation that those Jews who do not acquire their religion from the tradition of their group, quite generally do not get it elsewhere. The American civilization, be it remembered, is in itself largely secular. Such Jews then, as often as not, simply go through life without a sustained *Weltanschauung*, an organic ethical code, and patterns of ritual.

Beyond this, my life is enriched by the accumulated treasures of over three millennia of Jewish culture—a large literature in which I read extensively, not as an outsider might, but with a sense of belonging. I have the privilege of companionship with the great worthies of Jewish history.

There is at my disposal a second fund of folklore when I wish to spin tales to my children. Mine is literally a double past—the American and the Jewish. My horizons are distant, not in one direction but in two. I am twice anchored in traditions, and hence twice secured against the peril of being "unpossessed."

And because my Jewishness is something positive, anti-Semitism looms less large in my life than in that of many of my fellows. I am not hagridden by it as they are. To them it is the whole of what is otherwise a senseless identification; to me it is an unfortunate, undesired but apparently unavoidable incident in an inherently worth-while enterprise. Like them I am prepared to do anything I can to resist it. I, too, man the walls but in defense of shrines, libraries, and family altars as much as of jobs, legal rights, and memberships in golf clubs. And I know that while in the event of defeat, much will be taken from me, my Jewish heritage will still remain to sustain me and give me direction. The dejudaized Jews, on the other hand, recognize quite clearly that they will be left with nothing. Little wonder that their preoccupation with anti-Semitism approaches a hysteria.

I am furthermore quite confident that by virtue of my attitudes I am less susceptible than escapist Jews to infection by self-contempt. I am undeniably exposed to the same psychic influences that play over them, but in my case, participation in and appreciation of the Jewish tradition operates as an immunizing element. I am not tempted to flight from myself, nor bitter, because I know in advance that it will prove futile. I cannot despise my identity; it is associated with a process which I enjoy and respect. Not the least of the significances for me of a meaningful Judaism is its contribution to my mental health.

But is not the survivalist program provocative of anti-Semitism? Is it not self-ghettoization? Does it not set Jews apart and by their differential behaviors incite the hostility of non-Jews? In response, two observations must be recorded. In the first instance, I do not envisage, nor have I practiced, withdrawal from the general life of America. While to me the Jewish religion is my first and only religion, the Jewish culture, on the other hand, is secondary to the general American civilization. It is an additional supplementary tradition, interest in which does not in the least militate against full participation in the common political and spiritual life of our country.

And it is barking up the wrong tree to ascribe the waxing and waning of anti-Semitic moods to the attitudes of Jews toward their Judaism. Prejudice against Jews is the result of deep-seated social forces. The anti-Semite is not an anti-Semite because he observes that Jews maintain their traditional Sabbath or sing their ancient folk songs in their homes. Nor is he more kindly disposed toward them if he learns that they have departed from the ways of their fathers. He feels as he does about Jews perhaps because a bias has been communicated to him early in life in his home, church, or school; perhaps because he has met and resented their economic competition; perhaps because someone in his society is deliberately fanning group tensions to divert his attention from basic social maladjustments; perhaps because he is a frustrated human being or because his society

97

is sick and he is casting about for someone upon whom to vent his irritation, someone to blame for whatever is wrong in his life or that of his country. It should be noted that the fury of the pogrom, physical or verbal, beats equally on traditionalist and assimilationist Jews. In brief, any number of factors may be the causes of the emergence or intensification of an anti-Semitic mood. The relations of Jews to their Jewish heritage is rarely, if ever, one of them.

IV

Is it practicable, this prospectus of two civilizations, the primary American and the secondary Jewish? Identification with Judaism as a credal communion raises no issues of feasibility in our minds. We are accustomed to the circumstance that Americans will be identified with minority churches. After all, every religious denomination in our own country is of such a character vis-à-vis the total population. But can a person live happily, without stress and strain, in two cultures?

If I may judge from my experience—and that of many Jews who share my viewpoint—the program is amazingly undifficult of execution. Let it be recalled that to me the American tradition is my primary heritage. I acknowledge only one political allegiance—to America. English is my first language, and that of my children. I was educated in the public schools of my community. The history of America is my history. I mean it when I sing "land where my fathers died." But Jewish history is my background too. Lincoln and Jefferson are my heroes together with Rabbi Akiba and Moses Maimonides. The four get along in my imagination most companionably. When I read Van Wyck Brooks's *Flowerng of New England*, it is in my own literary past that I am being instructed. I have studied Spiegel's *Hebrew Reborn* with the same sense of identification. Picasso's "Blue Boy" and Anton Schutz's etchings of New York adorn the same walls in my home on which hang the works of Struck, Lilien, and Joseph Margulies. I sing Negro spirituals, American ballads, and Hasidic or Palestinian folk songs with equal vigor and tonelessness. On the Fourth of July I set off fireworks and attempt to transmit to my children my appreciation of the significance of the holiday. With equal earnestness I kindle Hanukkah lights and discuss the meaning of that festival. At no time am I conscious of strain or incompatability between the two worlds. I move from one to the other with such naturalness that I am scarcely aware of the change in spiritual locale.

The whole process is facilitated immensely by the essential sympathy in spirit between the two traditions. Both are democratic. Both emphasize the worth of the individual and his right to freedom. In both there is passionate devotion to the ideal of social justice. And the vision of the more abundant life is a secularized parallel of the ancient Jewish dream of the Kingdom of God on earth.

Incidentally it should be noted that tacitly, at least, America approves, or to put it more modestly, has no quarrel with my enterprise. For it is the essence of our political theory that the state exists so that the individual may find fulfillment where his conscience and intelligence direct. If then some American citizens believe that they require a special religion for their salvation, or divergent cultural expressions for their self-realization, America offers no objection—provided always that the differential interests do not operate adversely to the shared political and cultural life. Indeed, in a very real sense, it can be said that it is to this end that American democracy exists.

V

Any program for the Jewish group must, as I have already indicated, meet a twofold test of acceptability: the welfare of the Jewish group, the welfare of America. It is my conviction that the pattern I follow measures up better than all its alternatives not only to the first criterion but to the second as well. America, I am certain, is best served by its Jews when they strive to exploit the special resources of their group.

If the only effects of such a course were to bolster the shaken morale of the Jews and to enrich their personalities with the treasures of a second heritage, the whole effort would have justified itself from the point of view of American interest. Quite obviously America will be benefited if its Jews who constitute one segment of its citizenry respect themselves, if they are psychically adjusted rather than disaffected and if, in addition, they are richer rather than poorer in spirit.

But beyond all such considerations there is a larger promise in this cultural dualism and its analogues. It is out of differences meeting in reciprocal understanding on a shared soul that cultures bloom most luxuriantly. History is replete with precedent for this statement. The age of Pericles, the Renaissance, the eras of Chaucer and Shakespeare, were all, in no slight measure, the consequence of the cross-fertilization of civilizations. The botanist has long known that plants grow best when they pollinate one another. He has for many centuries been doing deliberately what Nature had been wont to do hit or miss. Those of us who are devoted to the ideal of an American flower could, it would seem, properly follow his precedent. We ought preserve both the common ground of government, language, and culture in which all groups share, and also the second diversities, and then as a matter of planned policy arrange for their mutual meeting. Out of such husbandry of the spirit may well emerge a cultural life richer than any the human past has known heretofore.

I believe in the attainability of this objective. I believe further that Judaism has its contribution to make to the great fruition which is to be. This is the final and climactic reason for a program dedicated to the preservation of the Jewish tradition on the American scene.

CHAPTER 6

AMERICAN JEWRY'S COMING OF AGE

TWENTY-FIVE years is not a very long time in the life of any community. It is, however, a long time when one considers the transformations which have taken place during that period with American Jewry. For in the past quarter of a century American Jewry has become of age. A group which was preponderantly immigrant, its roots set in lands across the seas, has become in the course of two and a half decades, overwhelmingly native born. A population large segments of which were as yet unacclimatized to American life, without possession of the tongue of the land, without intimate knowledge of its social practices and precedents, has achieved a virtually total Americanization.

The whole development of American Jewry during the past quarter of a century has moveover been from heterogeneity to homogeneity. A quarter of a century ago the American Jewish community was sharply divided between the Sephardic and German elements on one side, long resident in the country, highly Americanized in outlook and patterns of living; and on the other hand, the great masses of East European Jews, still new to the American scene.

So complete a homogeneity has been achieved among us in so short a time span that it is today virtually impossible to detect, on the basis of external behavior or internal attitudes, exactly what our individual antecedents may have been.

This quarter century, then, has proved long enough for a major transformation in the nature of American Jewry. It is long enough, certainly, to serve as the basis of judgments concerning Jewish cultural accomplishments, concerning the extent to which American Jews are realizing the cultural potentialities resident in their situation and themselves; long enough for an appraisal of the record of American Jewry in the realm of Jewish culture. My view, and I shall state it boldly at the outset, is that our group has been far less creative in the area of Jewish arts and letters than might have been expected; that, amidst circumstances which should have spelled great spiritual fertility on our part, we have been not entirely, but largely, sterile.

Most recently I had occasion to read a careful study of the factors responsible for the brilliant flowering of the Jewish community during the golden age in Spain. The student who traced the influences which co-operated to make possible this great outpouring of genius and talent conceded at the very outset that the creative spirit is always and ultimately unpredictable. The soil, he argued, may be right for productivity of the spirit, yet none may be forthcoming. The climate may seem altogether favorable to artistic expression, yet that self-expression may not realize itself.

But, having granted the truth that environment of and by itself does not guarantee genius, the student then proceeded to list the environmental factors which at least served to encourage and stimulate self-expression on the part of that great medieval Jewry. Among these he included the following as of greatest moment. The community of Spain was for a long time politically unrepressed, and exempt from external pressures and persecution. It was, moreover, possessed of large economic recourses. In consequence, it contained a leisure class free to live the cultural life and to foster it. Again, Spanish Jewry was set in the midst of an enlightened, culturally sensitive society. The old Yiddish epigram, *"Wie es christelt sich, so judelt sich,"* "like Christian, like Jew," applied to Jewish communities then as at the present. Any Jewry which resides in the midst of a retarded Gentile populace is likely to be dragged down to its level. On the other hand, a Jewish community which is stimulated and challenged by its environment is likely to reflect in its own vigor the intellectual vigors of the land of which it is a part. Furthermore, the Jews of Spain contained within themselves a patron class which was motivated by the ideal of lending encouragement to creative artists, and also a receptive mass public, an audience, both of large value in the development of cultural movements. Last of all, Spanish Jewry had behind it, and was propelled by, the momentum of a long tradition which included rich Biblical rabbinic and Gaonic elements. This was an influence of no slight significance. For no community is likely to pour itself out in literature, music, or art unless there is at the very least some tradition from which it can derive inspiration and stimulation.

It occurred to me, as I read this particular historical study,

that every one of the factors which served to evoke so colorful an efflorescence on the part of Spanish Jewry has long
been present on the American Jewish scene.

The American Jewish community, in the first instance,
has from its very founding enjoyed political security and
freedom. It has in the second place been possessed of considerable economic resources, sufficient certainly to finance
diverse and multiple cultural interests. Again, the American Jewish community like the Spanish is enveloped by
an atmosphere of cultural activity. It is surrounded on all
sides by a people interested in books, in art, and in literature.
The cultural life of America is variegated, vigorous, and
challenging both to individuals and minority groups. To
be sure, the medieval institution of patronage for learning
and esthetic expression exists no more. But modern society
has developed more than adequate substitutes. The American Jewish community, as well as interested Gentiles,
constitute a large audience for any author or artist. American Jewry possesses all the antecedent elements of a historical character necessary to cultural creativity in the present.

Consider the stuff which has gone into the making of
the minds of Jewish Americans. There is, first of all community: the general and shared cultural life of America,
in which Jews have participated very widely and to which
they are totally responsive. There is, in the second place,
a complex of streams of influence deriving from the lands
of origins of Jews in this country. Among these is to be
numbered a Sephardic cultural strain. Broader and deeper,
because of the number of persons involved, is an American
Jewish heritage, Germanic in character. There are thousands

of Jewish households in this country in which Schiller, and Goethe, and Heine, are part of the cultural background. Present in the thought life of American Jews are also certain Slavonic elements, brought by East European Jews from their native lands to the New World. Over and beyond all these, stands the whole body of the specifically Jewish tradition—Scripture, the literatures of the Haskalah and of Zionism, which have also touched the American Jewish personality, the Yiddish heritage, and, more recently, the new Palestinian. Our Jewry, in brief, does not lack for cultural background. This leads me at last to the central point of my thesis: all the conditions are present which any objective analysis would require for a cultural outpouring on the part of the four million Jews of America. Yet, I think, any sober and dispassionate judgment of the record of the American Jewish community in the course of the past quarter of a century leads to the sad conclusion that it has been far less creative along specifically Jewish lines than might have been expected in the light of the favoring circumstances which I have enumerated.

For the purpose of this analysis I shall adapt a procedure employed by Professor Sorokin in his volume, *The Crisis of Our Age*. In attempting to define the quality and temper of any given society, Professor Sorokin examines statistically first the actual output of books, music, philosophy, and art of that society. By this key Professor Sorokin hopes to determine the basic *Stimmung* of a particular society at a particular time.

As a basis for my own investigation I have selected a listing of novels of Jewish interest in the English language.

This catalogue was drawn up by a group interested in recommending literature of a Jewish character to American Jewish readers. It does not pretend to be complete or exhaustive. It can, however, be assumed with safety to be fairly representative of Anglo-Jewish fiction. Certainly, it contains almost every important novel in the English tongue bearing on Jewish life.

This list upon close examination invites some very interesting inferences. The whole list comprises 62 titles. Of these, 38, or well more than half, represent translations from the Yiddish, the Hebrew, or the German; 4 of these books were written by Christians, including one Jewish convert to Christianity; 4 were written by British Jews; 3 by American Jews but by American Jews whose background and education are European throughout. Of the entire list of 62 titled, only 13 are of authentic and indisputable American Jewish origin. Nor is it irrelevant to add that of these thirteen, none, in my judgment, is even of the first magnitude—none, for example, approximates in importance the Joseph cycle by Thomas Mann, which is also included in the catalogue.

The facts interpret themselves, and that none too happily. If the novel is used as a criterion—and there is no reason against such a procedure—the conclusion is inescapable that the American Jew has failed very generally to utilize the opportunities and to realize the potentialities for cultural creativity resident within himself and his situation.

Analogous studies in related fields would, I believe, yield similar results. American Jewry has done poorly in poetry, music, drama, the dance, and the graphic arts. There is, for example, much significant verse of recent publication in Hebrew and Yiddish. There is almost none in English. The contrast between Palestinian and American Jewry is moreover too obvious to require statistical analysis. The Palestinian community, one-ninth the size of the American and infinitely poorer in resources, has been vastly the more creative in almost every field of cultural interest.

At a time when the whole democratic process and spirit are fighting for survival, and when the Jewish group finds itself hemmed in by extraordinary pressures, the tone, temper, and vigor of our cultural life may seem to be relatively unimportant. Yet I am convinced that the failure of the past twenty-five years—not a total failure, to be sure, but certainly a failure in large part—has very large significance and consequence for the American Jewish community.

We must bear in mind that it is the avowed purpose of Judaism to enrich and ennoble Jews, to enhance their lives with religious insights, ethical values, and cultural richnesses. A Judaism which is meagerly creative is transparently fulfilling its self-assigned function only inadequately.

What is more, the readiness of Jews to live as Jews must over a long range be directly proportionate to their judgment of the worth of Jewishness to their own lives. Obviously, a Jew who feels himself enriched and stimulated by Judaism, who senses that his intellectual horizons have been widened by it, will spontaneously be ready to identify himself with Jewish life. The failure of American Jewry to be culturally creative, therefore, is in effect an adverse vote against the continuance of the Jewish tradition on the American scene. To those to whom Jewish tradition is a matter of vital concern, this is no trivial consideration even in the midst of the large human crisis of our time.

In addition, Judaism and the Jewish group are potentially of large significance to American life. But the extent of that significance will be determined by the ability of the American Jewish community to make contributions in its own idiom to the total spiritual life of America as a whole. Jews, to be sure, can serve America simply as Americans. Another opportunity is open up to them as well—a service as American Jews. The exploitation of this differential opportunity requires the creation in the English language and American idiom of Jewish music, and art, and literature, as a contribution to the shared cultural interests of America as a whole. By a paradox, which is ultimately no paradox, we are failing America in failing Judaism. Despite the fact, then, that we find ourselves under circumstances of crisis, when immediate and urgent problems bear upon us, these issues of cultural creativity remain of prime importance. On our disposition of them depends the self-realization of Judaism, the readiness of Jews to continue the Jewish enterprise, and their ability to fulfill themselves as Americans who are also Jewish Americans.

But how, in the light of all the favorable circumstances we have enumerated, shall we account for the fact that there has been so little of cultural self-expression on the part of the American Jewish community? To me it would seem that there are five fundamental factors which together account for Jewish cultural sterility on the American scene.

The first of these is a fallacy of definition, a misconception of the nature of Judaism under which the American Jewish community has long labored. Until most recently the influence of German-Jewish theorizing concerning the nature of a Jewish identity was very powerful among American Jews. The predominant motif of that thinking was that the Jews represented a credal communion only; that being a Jew was analogous to, let us say, being a Methodist; and that the content of Judaism was no larger than the content of Methodism. Once, however, the Jewish identity was defined exclusively in terms of religion, only such Jewish enterprises became legitimate as dealt with or expressed faith attitudes, ethics, or rituals. All interests of a cultural character at once became inappropriate to Jewish life.

I would not be misunderstood at this point. I am a convinced religionist. Yet, this definition of the Jewish identity exclusively in terms of credal affirmation has been, it seems to me, both a blunder in logic and a factor contributing to the cultural sterility of the Jewish group. For if we Jews constitute a credal communion, and a credal communion only, then literature, unless it be literature of a religious character, simply does not belong in Jewish life; nor music, nor art, unless they, too, are of the synagogue. In brief, there has been present among American Jews a state of mind which has inhibited cultural expression largely because it proceeded from assumptions under which such cultural expression was regarded as irrelevant and inappropriate to Judaism.

A second influence adverse to Jewish culture flowed inevitably from this fallacy of definition. Once Judaism was defined exclusively in terms of religious affirmation, that Jew who happened to find himself incapable of such affirmation was led to consider himself a virtual outsider to the Jewish community. I hold no brief for agnosticism or atheism among Jews, and I will argue vigorously with and against the Jewish agnostic and the Jewish atheist. I am convinced that religion is not only a legitimate aspect of Jewish life, but also indispensable to it. Yet, as it happens, not every Jew shares my views. After all, the strain on faith in modern times has been very heavy. Any number of Jews have like their Christian brethren been unequal to it. And there are, in my opinion, other areas within Judaism beside religion. In consequence, I can see neither the justice nor the wisdom of ruling these people out of Jewry by implication. The sole effect of such an approach is to alienate thousands of Jews, some of them among the most sensitive, alert, and resourceful, from all areas of Jewish life, and so to inhibit in advance any impulse toward creativity in fields beside religion which might stir within them.

There is a third factor which also to some degree is responsible for Jewish cultural sterility. I refer to the widespread misreading of the future of Judaism in America. I think that many Jews twenty-five years or more ago expected the ultimate extinction through assimilation of Judaism in America. That expectation is unfortunately with us still. But given such a prediction, all efforts on behalf of Judaism necessarily are marked with an air of futility. There is, after all, no point in putting time, energy, and devotion into an enterprise which sooner or later is destined to liquidation.

Side by side with this miscalculation of the future of Judaism went a widespread misinterpretation of the nature of America. Under the old melting-pot theory, all cultural diversities, it was expected, would be obliterated. America would achieve a homogeneous Anglo-Saxonimity, with only variations of religion to disturb the indifferentiated social scene. Such an outlook as to Americanism was, needless to say, scarcely conducive to efforts within a minority tradition.

A strong sense of the irrelevance of Jewishness to the lives of American Jews has been still another inhibitant to Jewish creativity. It has been taken almost as axiomatic among many American Jews that while Jews might out of piety and devotion live a Jewish life, they could, if they so elected, manage to achieve a full existence without such interests. Judaism therefore, for many Jews, has been invested with an air of the superfluous, the dispensable.

The next contributing factor has been the breakdown of Jewish education on the American scene. After two thousand years of the successful and continuous transmission of a heritage through a particular social machinery, that mechanism suddenly proved inadequate when transferred to the New World. It is both futile and unfair to blame the East European Jew for the mistakes which he made in the Jewish education of his children. After all, the *cheder* had functioned satisfactorily abroad. Quite naturally then he assumed that the same devices would function here. Nor in his preoccupation with the language of a strange land, and with the tasks of adjusting himself to a new world and of making a livelihood in it, could he be expected to give too much critical attention to the less immediate problems of education. Whatever the causes and the responsibilities, the tragic fact is that virtually whole generations of American

Jews were left without any significant introduction to the historic Jewish tradition. The result is, as might have been anticipated, that a people which does not know its culture does not attempt to find expression in it.

Last of all, there has been on the part of the American Jewish community a serious neglect of the obligation to provide organized encouragement to Jewish cultural values. Let it be borne in mind—and this is a significant factor in the whole picture—that Jews on the American scene represent a cultural minority; that for them the predominant American civilization is their first civilization. To the majority culture they turn naturally both as a matter of necessity and of obligation. Jewish cultural interests (I do not now refer to the Jewish religion which is, of course, the first and only religion of Jews) must assume a secondary role. But if a people is to be creative in its secondary cultural tradition, two prerequisites are required: First, that the minority community shall forge the instruments whereby the creative artist shall be encouraged to labor in the minority tradition and whereby a receptive public shall be provided for him. Second, that there shall be some place in the world where that same culture shall exist in a primary, not in a secondary role.

In providing both these prerequisites American Jewry has been derelict in its duty. It has done too little in a systematic fashion to foster and encourage Jewish culture on the American scene. It has made no sustained attempt to utilize and exploit those outpourings of cultural creativity, which Palestine, the site of a primary Hebraism, has already manifested. It has allowed *Bialik* and *Achad Ha'am,* for example, to go largely untranslated, a neglect which is an offense against both the Jewish spirit and the human. Indeed, it is apparently nobody's business to make available to American Jews what their Palestinian brothers are creating on their behalf. For all the cultural productivity of Palestine, American Jewry has been too lethargic and too disorganized to draw upon it systematically for its own internal enrichment.

The total effect of all these adverse factors is a general sterility, a cancellation of the favorable influences. And that sterility has been cumulative. The less cultural productivity, the less of value Jews see in their Judaism, and the less it stimulates them to contribute to it. And so on, in a kind of descending spiral of Jewish vigor and will.

Our record then during the past quarter century has been largely one of failure, of an inability to realize large potentialities. It has, however, a brighter side. There is abundant reason to believe that the adverse factors are, one and all, now at least in the process of neutralization. There is occasion for the hope that they will yet be so completely neutralized that creativity will break forth richly from our midst.

American Jewry is now beginning to recover from the fallacious definition under which it has operated for so long a time. It is beginning to recognize that there is more to being a Jew than theological affirmation, important as that may be; that culture too is part of a Jewish identity.

Again, the position of Judaism within American life has been clarified. Indeed, the nature of Americanism in general has been clarified as a result of reflection during most recent decades. The melting-pot notion is going. Thoughtful Americans no longer envisage the future of their society in a boiling down of its diversities into a common, undifferentiated uniformity. Rather they envisage America in terms of cultural pluralism. That term is so often misunderstood that we must pause over it for a moment. It does not imply, as is sometimes asserted, the Balkanization of America, either politically, linguistically, or in any other fashion. It assumes that all Americans will speak English as their first tongue, will participate equally and alike in the common American political, economic, social, and cultural patterns. Beyond this area of shared interests, however, it allows for minority cultural concerns. For us Jews, the vision of cultural pluralism means this: that we shall share in the American civilization with all other Americans; that we shall of course have no political allegiance except to the American commonwealth; but that we shall in addition maintain not only our traditional Jewish religion, but our traditional Jewish culture as well. And it is hoped that out of our second culture and that of other groups, all operating upon the shared American life, there shall emerge for America reciprocal stimulations and enrichments, a diversity of color and of idea, so that out of diversity moving over unity the American spirit as a whole may be the stronger and fairer.

In the light of such anticipations, Jewish cultural interests become clearly relevant both to our revised definition of Judaism and to our deeper understanding of Americanism.

Judaism, which heretofore has seemed to some so largely irrelevant, has of late acquired real and immediate cogency.

We know now that the Jew can use his Jewishness. There may be some question as to whether he has got to take it whether he wants it or not, but that he can use it is now generally admitted on all sides. Judaism, we have discovered, is good for the Jew; good for his psychic health; good in that it can enrich his personality; good in that it can make him the source of special contributions to America as a whole.

Among other things the past quarter of a century has witnessed a slow recovery from the blunders which were made in educational procedures. New techniques have been evolved. A new teaching personnel has come into being, thoroughly American, thoroughly adapted to the American scene and the American child. The process of adult education, interrupted for years, is now falteringly beginning to manifest itself once again.

And at long last we are beginning to get the foreshadowings, the symptoms of a recognition on the part of the Jewish community of its obligation systematically to foster Jewish cultural interests. First steps have been made in community centers and synagogues for the organized encouragement of Jewish cultural expression. It is only a beginning which we have had so far in this direction. But even this is something. And we are starting too to utilize more extensively those outpourings of the intellect and of the heart which are the output of Palestine, the one Jewish community in the world which is Jewish without the necessity or the obligation of being something else first with most of its time and energy.

In sum, discouraging as is the picture, it is not without

its brighter side. And the trend is at last turning strongly in the right direction.

In the analogy which was suggested between the golden age of Spain and our own situation, there is one consideration which I have, for expository purposes, withheld until this point. It is true that in the tenth, eleventh, and twelfth centuries, under circumstances very strongly analogous to our own, the Jewish community of Spain gave birth to poets of the first magnitude, great metaphysicians and philosophers, historians, legalists, Biblical scholars, and so on. All of that is true, but the circumstance still to be considered is this: it took two hundred years for the Spanish Jewish community to begin to create. For it was in the early eighth century that the Jews of Spain, reduced to slavery by the Visigothic kings, were emancipated by the Moslem conquest. It was not until the tenth century, two hundred years later, that poets, Biblical scholars, legalists, and philosophers manifested themselves.

It is my hope, indeed it is my judgment, that we shall not have to wait two centuries before we realize the opportunities and the potentialities implicit within our condition. We are more fortunate than the Spanish Jews in that we in America have no long bondage from which we must recuperate. To be sure, the spirit matures slowly and manifests itself in its own good time. It can be encouraged but not forced. Yet the signs and omens are already favorable. I can see no reason why we should not achieve a great flowering of Jewish culture even within the next generation provided that we are wise enough to perceive certain truths and to act in their light.

117

We must win through to and proceed on a valid and creative definition of Judaism as something larger than religion alone; we must recognize that there is a legitimate role and a useful function for Jewish culture in the American scheme of things; we must become aware of the relevance of Jewish interests to the lives of American Jews; we must overtake the breakdown in the Jewish educational process; and we must give organized encouragement within the American Jewish community to Jewish creativity, stimulating it furthermore by the systematic utilization of Palestinian cultural creativity.

The effectiveness of Judaism, the destiny of the Jewish group in America, will be determined in no slight measure by whether we are wise in husbanding the resources at our disposal and in marshaling them toward a great growth of the Jewish spirit. At the same time our worth to America not as Americans but as *Jewish* Americans will also be directly contingent upon us.

No two objectives, it seems to me, could be more challenging, more stimulating, and inherently more worth while than these: to preserve the Jewish heritage by enriching the content of Jewish life, and to enrich America by enriching Judaism.

CHAPTER 7

INDIGNATION—A LOST JEWISH VIRTUE

EW HUMAN faculties are unique to man. To be sure no
animal reasons as man does, in terms of ideas or concepts; or possesses a moral sense, an awareness of right and
wrong. But so far as feelings go men and animals seem to
share most of them. Animals love and hate as we do. They
are content or angry. Some reveal a desire for possession.
Some further show traces of esthetic impulses, of a sensitivity of the beautiful. And there are even in a few of the
highest mammals that instinct which makes the scientist
or novelist—the instinct of curiosity.

But one emotion animals do not and cannot feel. They
cannot be indignant. Angry, yes; indignant, never. Nor
is it hard to understand why. One need only to look at the
word, indignation, in terms of its origin. For the word comes
from the Latin, as a compound of the prefix *in* meaning
not, and *dignus* meaning worthy. Indignation is, therefore,
the resentment roused in us by the experience of that which
is not worthy. But an awareness of worth is something
intellectual or moral, hence man alone is capable of it.

Indignation is then the badge of man, one of the most

honorable of human traits. Judaism is a religion of love. Yet its most heroic figures were men of great indignation. Consider that meek man—Moses; what a capacity for indignation was his, indignation against the taskmaster beating the Jewish slave, indignation against his people worshiping the Golden Calf. Consider all the prophets after him—from Elijah to Malachi. Consider Christianity—for though Christianity started out to portray Jesus as the incarnation of pure love, it quickly gave up the attempt. It could not keep its picture of him moral unless it included in his make-up indignation also.

Indeed there is no social gain, from the destruction of feudalism and human slavery to the establishment of social security in our time, which has not, so to speak, been sparked by indignation.

And as for us as individuals, we would indeed be in a bad way were it not for this emotion. A human being if he is going to live at all, let alone respect himself, cannot take insult or injury passively. Now our reason cannot always be trusted to resist affront or attack. For, as Bergson says, one can always reason with reason. One can always tell himself that it is wiser to swallow the insult or not notice the slap on the face. This then is the supreme function of indignation in our lives: to break the deadlock of the mind and the paralysis of the will.

It follows from all this that the absence of indignation from a person's make-up is a very bad sign. It means in the end that he lacks a sense of worth, that he does not respect himself. And the person who does not respect himself will not only be stepped on by everybody but is in addition ripe for a psychiatrist. The one thing a human being must have for the health of his spirit is a vigorous self-respect.

One more word about indignation in the abstract. So far as its causes go, it falls into three distinct classifications. There is, first of all, the indignation of principle. Falsehood and injustice, no matter by whom committed, or against whom, of and by themselves evoke indignation in the morally sensitive person.

Sometimes, however, indignation derives from the *source* of an action. When a religious hypocrite participates in public worship we have no quarrel with what he is saying. On the contrary, he is saying very beautiful and very true things. But we are likely to be furious because he, of all people, has no right to have such sentiments on his lips.

And sometimes indignation is a matter of the person to whom something is done. It is true that Abraham Lincoln was an extraordinarily ugly man and yet it is still painful to remember that he was called a baboon. Any president of the United States deserves deference—and particularly Lincoln.

But sometimes it happens that in a given situation all the causes for indignation are present at the same time. Lies and injustice are propagated; they are propagated by base people and against good persons. Then one should expect a hurricane of indignation, a howling storm of it. There should be an explosion, and if there is none, something is very wrong somewhere.

Here ends theory. We now come to *tachlis,* to practical matters.

There are all sorts of reactions which Jews exhibit when

they encounter anti-Semitism. Fright is perhaps the most common. A stunned incredulity is another. An impulse to hide or run away a third. Some Jews when they run into prejudice immediately begin to condemn Jews as responsible for it, not themselves, of course, but all other Jews; there are other Jews who respond by repudiating Judaism, as though our faith, morality, and ritual were at fault.

They exhibit, then, all sorts of reactions to anti-Semitism. They are, however, almost never indignant about it. Decent Gentiles may be, but not Jews. And yet that is the emotion most clearly in order. For in anti-Semitism there is every reason for righteous anger you can think of. Anti-Semitism is in the first place a matter of monstrous lies and brutal injustice. You know and I know perfectly well that what the anti-Semite says is false from A to Z. We Jews are *not* engaged in international conspiracies. Our boys are *not* slackers in this or any other war. And what, pray, is the anti-Semite trying to accomplish: to intimidate decent people, to deprive them of their freedom and rights, to break their hearts and, if possible, their necks. If ever there was an occasion for indignation, here it is. For anti-Semitism is intellectually and morally an offense that stinks to heaven.

And who are the anti-Semites? The mentally sick, the embittered, the frustrated, the sadists. And if they are not sick, then they are worse, they are unprincipled and conscienceless. It is part of my Jewish faith to believe in the dignity of man; but our ancestors who esteemed man so highly, were also realistic about him. They knew that there are men who are wicked, and others who are fools. Such is the anti-Semite. If honest he is either sick or a fool; if dishonest he is a mean, nasty, unscrupulous person. To be sure, the anti-Semite is himself a creature of circumstance. He has been made into what he is by environment and personal misfortunes. He is someone to be understood and pitied. But, as Samuel Johnson once put it, "When a madman armed with a club comes into my bedchamber he is a pitiable person. But first I knock him down and take his club and then I pity him."

And we Jews have a right to be indignant. We are too good for that kind of treatment. All through history we have been a constructive, a humane, a civilizing force. And that we are as a whole today. There are exceptions of course —Jews who are unethical, and others who are quite unappetizing socially. I am not happy over such Jews, not because of what Gentiles may say, but because I expect much—the best and highest from Jews. As descendants of the prophets, pupils of the sages, we cannot be content with moral mediocrity. But that is a matter for our own consciences. Meantime it is a fact that vulgarians and corner-cutters are no more common among us than among other groups, and much less common than might have been expected in the light of the persecution and the disabilities that have always been our lot.

And as for the mass of Jews—I am deliberately forgetting the Einsteins and the Bergsons—they are decent, honorable, kindly people, very good citizens and very well behaved. When I think of what our people has been and what it is now, and then when I think of the kind of riffraff who insult us, there is only one phrase that expresses my feelings—the *Hutzpah,* the brazen, unmitigated *Hutzpah.*

Now indignation, we just observed, is necessary to action. Being deficient in it, we acquit ourselves very badly when we meet anti-Semitism. And by we I mean not only individuals, but also our civic defense agencies—the American Jewish Committee, the American Jewish Congress, the Anti-Defamation League.

Self-defense is a law of all living things, recognized by morality and law alike. But not for us Jews. Let us run into anti-Semitism and we do not defend ourselves—we play Hamlet, we engage in debates with ourselves and one another. Is it not wiser, we ask, to ignore the incident. Perhaps by recognizing it, we may give it publicity and so put bees into otherwise beeless bonnets. Words, not deeds! This is our regular response to anti-SEMITISM. And these words are addressed, generally, not to the anti-Semites, but to one another.

Do I seem to be exaggerating? Then let us think of Boston where, recently, for over a year, Jews were terrorized by hoodlums, and where the Jewish community did not so much as raise a finger in its own behalf. Or let us consider still another circumstance—our tendency to depend on Gentiles rather than ourselves for defense. It has become almost a standard belief among Jews that resistance to anti-Semitism comes with better grace and efficacy from non-Jews than from us. And so in any "situation" we wait for Gentiles to step in. And if they do not do so spontaneously, we organize them to that end. This policy, toward which I was long sympathetic, has come of late to seem to me gravely abused. In the first place, it is unnatural. When an innocent man is waylaid by thugs, he welcomes the assistance of all law-abiding citizens. But he does not stand idle in the meantime. He defends himself. Again our tendency to rely on Gentile help, and sometimes on Gentile "fronts," has created a peculiar problem. Most of the Gentiles who rally to our aid are pure idealists. But some are our friends only because it pays. And we are never quite sure which is which. The sad truth is that we are in danger of creating a new and profitable business, the business of being a professional friend of Jews, a merchant trading in Jewish fears.

The upshot of all this is—it is sickening to confess—that the Jews of America are taking anti-Semitism lying down, on the ground when they ought to be on their feet, fighting back.

I have heard of subway cars crowded with Jews who listened, eyes downcast, unmoving, ashamed as though they were criminals caught in some crime, while some anti-Semite—very often a professional Jew baiter—shouted anti-Semitic remarks.

In Boston, and here too, in New York, and elsewhere as well, one refrain runs through almost all stories of anti-Semitic incidents: "And so, they said to me, are you a Jew, and I ran." And there are our children—free-born native Americans. Why, their fathers, the ghetto guttersnipes of the East Side a generation ago, showed more spunk. When they were attacked as Jews by gangs of hoodlums, they had at least the common decency to organize their own gangs in self-defense.

But I have drifted from the main point. I am speaking of self-defense, and that is only half the story. It is no secret to you that anti-Semitism is the first cause of attack upon America and its democracy. The Jew who takes it passively is guilty of more than submission to personal indignity. He is morally guilty of treason to our country and to mankind.

I do not wish to imply that we Jews are in for an anti-Semitic storm against which we had better brace ourselves. I do not know what tomorrow may bring—no one knows. It is my hunch—which I present for whatever it is worth—that so far as anti-Semitism goes, the future will not be much different from the past. If, as seems likely, postwar problems—demobilization, reconversion, unemployment—will operate to intensify anti-Semitism, the victory of democracy, the camaraderie of Jews and Gentiles in the armed forces will, I am certain, work the other way. I am not suggesting either that we Jews go through life with chips on our shoulders, forgetting the millions of decent non-Jews, making an issue of every random situation, of every chance remark, calling in the policeman or getting into brawls at the slightest provocation. Coercion is something to be invoked only after every device of reason and persuasion has been exhausted.

Finally, I am not so naïve as to suppose that all we need do to solve the problem of anti-Semitism is to get indignant.

That there is a solution, I am convinced. I do not propose to present it at length, but let me give the chapter headings.

A basic cure for anti-Semitism requires at least the following seven measures:

1. A sustained campaign of education against all form of group prejudice.

2. The encouragement of friendships and co-operation on a plane of equality between Jews and non-Jews as individuals and as organized bodies.

3. The preservation and enlargement of political democracy.

4. The achievement of a greater measure of economic justice for all.

5. The establishment of codes of Fair Employment and Fair Social Practice, both state and national, with agencies empowered to enforce them.

6. The promulgation of legislation, state and federal, which, while protecting legitimate freedom of expression, would make it a crime to incite hatred against a group because of race, creed, or color.

7. The development of increased unity and co-ordination among Jewish civic defense agencies. It is well to remember that the Boston debacle was fostered by Jewish communal disorganization.

These are the true answers to our problem. We ought to work very hard on them. But in the meantime, let us be sure of one thing. Whenever anti-Semitism raises its head and we are certain it is the real thing, after every device of reason and persuasion has been tried and has failed, then let us hit at it as hard as we can. Let us, as lawyers say, throw the book at it in every way permitted by the Constitution, the Ten Commandments, and the Marquis of Queensberry.

Although such tactics may not stop the anti-Semite—

though I wager it will exert a salutary influence on him too—it will in any case be very good for American democracy and very good for our self-respect.

But the core of our question still remains untouched. Why are Jews deficient in indignation? Because, of course, they lack as Jews a sense of worth.

You see, too many of us Jews have no God and no Torah, no Jewish knowledge and no Jewish practices—only the penalties of being Jews. We never enjoy Judaism—we only suffer for it and even that not heroically. The Jew who knows Judaism has his head and heart too full of positive healthful values ever to be invaded by self-contempt. But the Jew who is a hollow shell, a Jewish Zero, a Hebraic cipher, a vacuum, is flooded inevitably with hostile notions about Jews. The anti-Semite convinces him. He comes to doubt his work and to despise Judaism, Jews, and even himself.

How then can he wax indignant? When libels about Jews come to his ears, his reaction is not anger; he assumes that they are true, not of him, of course, but of other Jews. Cursed with a sense of inferiority, convinced that everything Gentile is better than anything Jewish, sick to death with that dread disease, Goyitis, he is incapable of being offended by anything a Gentile does no matter who the Gentile or how unjust the act.

There are many advantages which Jews may derive from a knowledge and love of Judaism. It can give them a high, clear religious faith. It can supply them with a system of ethical values, personal and social, idealistic and practical at the same time. It can grace their lives with poetic observances and with the treasures of an ancient tradition. It can make them, in sum, nobler, stronger, better human beings and more valuable citizens.

But one service Judaism performs for Jews which is often overlooked: it is the first function of a human being to respect himself, to stand erect and foursquare before the world, to injure none, to help all, but to allow none to injure him—to be in sum, a man.

This is the last and climactic contribution of a living Judaism to the Jew—it delivers him from being a worm; it guarantees that he will be a man.

CHAPTER 8

THE RIGHT NOT TO BE A JEW

❋❋❋❋❋❋❋❋❋❋❋❋❋❋❋❋❋❋❋❋❋❋❋❋❋❋❋❋❋❋❋

THE POSITION of the modern Jew is radically different
from that of his medieval ancestors in his political
rights, economic opportunities, social acceptance, and his
access to the thought life of the land in which he lives.
Even in lands of persecution, the Jew is by no means so
isolated from the larger life of the scene in which he finds
himself as were his forefathers.

Among the points of differentiation between the modern
Jew and the medieval, one of the most significant lies in
the realm of internal attitudes. Our medieval ancestors
tended to take their Judaism, its theology, its morality, and
its system of ritual on authority. It never, or at most rarely,
occurred to them to challenge their tradition. They did
not feel, if they were at all typical of their time, that they
possessed the right to question what the past told them to
be true and desirable.

Across the span of the centuries it is not hard for us to
understand why that should have been so. In the first place,
the medieval Jew regarded the whole of his tradition as of
divine origin. Naturally enough he felt it a presumption to

impugn or to reject that which God had ordained for his salvation and for that of mankind. In addition, the Jew until recently lived in an entirely Jewish milieu. His viewpoints were confirmed rather than challenged by those with whom he came in contact. The full pressure of the ghetto and its social momentum co-operated to insure on his part a full and unquestioning conformity. In addition, the example of the Gentile world corroborated his acceptances. For it too acknowledged without reservations an authority, that of the Church and of its sacred writings.

It is scarcely necessary to point out how different in tone such an attitude is from that which prevails in the minds of most contemporary Jews. One need only observe the individual Jew of our day to recognize how free he feels to pass judgment on the whole of the Jewish tradition or any of its parts. Nor is it hard to understand whence this shift in viewpoint was derived. The older Jewish theology has, for many thousands and tens of thousands of Jews, broken down. There is no longer in their minds a supernatural sanction for the system of Jewish living. The modern Jew lives with and among Gentiles. He absorbs their ways of thinking and their modes of living. This contact with another system of existence necessarily shakes his Jewish routines. What is more, the Jew is no longer part of an integrated, unified Jewish group. He is now a Jewish atom flung off into space. He feels as a result that he must settle in his own mind what he will believe or disbelieve, what he will accept or reject. Among the forces which have modified the viewpoint of Jews so sharply in so short a time, one springs from what has happened to society generally.

The recent history of Western civilization has been marked by the struggle to emancipate the individual from authority. As part of that world, the Jew has been affected by the rise of the doctrine of the freedom of the individual conscience and the right of that conscience to determine for itself what is truth and what is error. As a result, the Jew feels today that as a citizen of the twentieth century he has the right to determine for himself his own attitude toward Judaism.

Thus it has come to pass that we, as Jews, feel free to reject the totality of the Jewish tradition or any single part of it. We may if we are so minded withdraw from participation in Jewish life, individual and collective. These are privileges which have come to us as persons born in our age.

But what most modern Jews fail to perceive is that the right to reject Judaism in whole or in part carries with it a prior obligation—the obligation first to understand. A Jew has the right to reject Jewish religious attitudes but not until first he has come to comprehend their logical validity and psychological values. He has the right, if he sees fit, to abandon traditional observances, but not until he has first made an effort to understand their place in the Jewish scheme of things. He is free to embark upon a deliberate policy of assimilation. But he owes it to himself, to the Jewish group and to mankind, first to evaluate the possible implications of his program and the grounds on which it is rejected by protagonists of Jewish survival.

We have spoken of an obligation to understand. Whence does this obligation spring? It is derived in the first place from simple realities. Although in theory a Jew may abandon his Judaism in its totality, if he is so minded, the fact remains that assimilation is for most Jews an impossibility. It is therefore obviously the part of wisdom to make certain of the possible value of Judaism before one consigns himself to a dubious existence midway between two groups.

Again, each human being desires to live a full and rich life. Thousands and tens of thousands of individuals throughout the centuries have insisted that Judaism endowed their lives with meaning, significance, and beauty. Unless then, a person is ready deliberately to choose the poorer life, he should first test that which he is tempted to discard. What is more, liberty of thought and conduct, if it is to mean anything at all, must be responsible. Freedom, too, should operate under moral constraints. And it is an abuse of liberty of thought to exercise the liberty without the thought. It should be borne in mind, last of all, that the precious things which men now enjoy are the products of the efforts of men who lived in days gone by. The latter labored and suffered that we as their children might possess the spiritual resources which are now at our disposal. Things that are good and true and beautiful in life have been created for us slowly and by intense sacrifice. It is a kind of spiritual waste, a wantonness of the spirit, to disregard the accumulated heritage of the past without first evaluating it cautiously and carefully.

The obligation resting upon the Jew to understand before he rejects is real enough. No Jew who has any respect for his own intellect, no Jew who wishes to live as rich a life as he can, no Jew with any sense of realism or with any

133

feeling of responsibility to the past of mankind and to its future, can avoid that responsibility.

It is possible, of course, that a Jew may come to understand and still reject. With such an individual, Judaism can have no quarrel. It must say to him, Go thy way in peace; we shall reason with each other again tomorrow. Judaism has no complaint against honest, intelligent, and informed rejection of itself. But Judaism does have a quarrel with the man who accepts no responsibility, who rejects Judaism without a proper understanding of it. It is in the last analysis not freedom of thought which endangers Jewish values, but the freedom which some people arrogate to themselves not to think at all.

From many points of view it is much easier to be a Jew today than it was four or five hundred years ago. For all the persecution of our time the Jew, even in the lands of darkest repression, enjoys now a measure of liberty and security such as the medieval Jew scarcely dared envisage. But from another point of view, ours is the heavier burden. In one respect at least our ancestors were more fortunate than we are. They accepted what was taught to them and their problem was at an end. Their minds were so conditioned that it never occurred to them to claim the right to accept or to reject faith in God, standards of morality, patterns of observance, and their identification with the Jewish group. The times have thrown us intellectually upon our own resources. We are driven, often against our will, to subject our Jewish heritage to bold inquiry. We are the children of the modern world, free to believe or disbelieve, to accept or reject as our reason determines—a glorious freedom. But we are also the heirs of an obligation which, difficult though it may be, is equally glorious —the obligation of understanding before judging. Of that responsibility let the Jews of our day be reminded, for their own sake, for the sake of the Jewish group and its future, and for the sake of mankind to whose spiritual resources Israel may have further contributions to make.

CHAPTER 9

COMMENTARY MAGAZINE *

IT IS NOW some five years since the American Jewish Committee launched *Commentary* magazine as a monthly
journal of Jewish life, letters, and opinion. The time would
be ripe in any event for an appraisal of the enterprise. But
it is not a sense of its appropriateness which impels the
evaluation I am about to attempt, but a conviction of its
urgency. For in the course of its career *Commentary* has
developed not only very considerable strengths which have
won for it admiration and friendship; it has come to dis-
play very considerable weaknesses also, negative and destructive traits which tend to neutralize the virtues and to
bring into question whether, on the balance, it is more
a benefit or detriment to American Judaism.

It is this, the darker side of *Commentary,* which is both
the occasion and the burden of this paper. The tenor of
what I have to say does not make me happy, especially
since I began as an ardent friend to this magazine. I was
among its charter subscribers. Quite unsolicited I made it
my business, when promising articles came my way, to

* Written in November, 1949.

136

direct them to *Commentary*. For at least two pieces published in its first year or so I served as a volunteer agent. I am naturally reluctant to admit that my friendship was misplaced.

And yet speak this piece I must. For the sake, in the first instance, of the magazine, the virtues it possesses, the promise implicit in it.

I doubt whether either the editors or the sponsoring Publications Committee representative of the American Jewish Committee are aware of the extent and bitterness of the hostility they have awakened in broad sectors of American Jewry, especially among informed and committed Jews.

But these, the Jewishly knowledgeable and ardent, are the largest, most interested and dependable of followers for a publication of Jewish interest, as contrariwise they can become, by very virtue of the firmness and fervor of their convictions, the most powerful and implacable of antagonists. In making enemies of its natural friends *Commentary*, I fear, is engaged in nothing less than undermining its own status, perhaps its existence.

Behind my concern over *Commentary* looms a larger, deeper anxiety, over the precarious position and uncertain prospects of Judaism in America.

There is, I believe, still a chance for the achievement of a vital Jewish religious, ethical, cultural, and communal life in this land, edifying and redemptive to us as individuals and through us to America, Israel, mankind. The chance, however, is slim and diminishes rapidly. The alternative is a dejudaized American Jewry, bereft of its God and Torah, its will to live and joy in life, a mass golem of five million persons kept alive only by the evil spell of anti-Semitism.

Against the grimness of this prospect, there is one inescapable criterion for any Jewish enterprise: its Jewish impact. What, we must ask, is its effect on Jewish morale and spirituality? Does it enhance or diminish in Jews their sense of the worthwhileness and hopefulness of the Jewish enterprise, their will to rethink and refashion Judaism into higher meaningfulness?

This is not to say that I expect a Jewish undertaking, in this instance a journal of Jewish opinion, to be in favor of survival blindly and unquestioningly, or to serve as a house organ for Jewish organizations, or to make itself a mouthpiece of causes simply because they lay claim to survivalist intentions. Nor is there anything in Jewish life, be it belief, value, or institution, too sacred for open, unsparing examination. Criticism of Judaism and a variety of viewpoints concerning it are not only legitimate, they are burning necessities. Indeed it is only in a searingly honest scrutiny of the Jewish condition, and radical and ruthless analyses of all proposals for its amelioration that hope may be reposed for any Jewish future at all, let alone a better one. It must be motivated by hope, not despair. It must be, if not immediately, then ultimately, constructive in intention. Even when it attacks or despises whatever in Jewish life is hateful or unlovely, its very hatred must be, like that of the prophets of old, an expression of an ultimate love.

It is then from a conviction, a hope and a sense of duty, that I speak this, believe me, very difficult and distasteful piece. The conviction is that *Commentary* magazine has disclosed itself as deficient in that ultimate love of Judaism without which no Jewish enterprise can be other than morally bankrupt. The hope is that this deficiency is not so deep-seated in the editors as to be irremediable. In any event, the duty to speak is clear. Is it not written:

"Thou shalt surely correct thy brother and not bear sin because of him."

Were *Commentary* some inconsequential sheet I would, no matter what its tenor, expend neither time nor energy on it.

The fact is, as I have already indicated, that it is a publication of many virtues. It is handsomely gotten up and appears regularly—no slight merit in a Jewish journal of opinion. It is expertly edited, at least on the technical level. To this fact, apparent on the face of things, I can testify from personal knowledge. I have seen the pieces which I steered *Commentary's* way both before and after public appearance. In each instance, the integrity of the content has been preserved, the form, however, had been skillfully recast. What is more, I have had the experience within the past year of rewriting an essay composed by one of my friends for publication in *Commentary*. In the form in which I had recast it it was, I assumed, passably fluent. I was left altogether admiring by the fashion in which the editor improved it by pointing up crucial sentences and rearranging materials. There is a talent peculiar to editing as to other arts. It was exhibited here.

But the excellences of this magazine run more than skin

deep. It provides a medium of expression for established American Jewish authors; it has developed new writers as well. It has succeeded in enlisting for the discussion of Jewish affairs men of talent, Jewish and Gentile alike, who otherwise would have stood aloof from such concerns. It has, on the whole, done a splendid job of reporting the Jewish scene, though considerably better as to Europe than Israel and immeasurably better as to both these than as to America. These reportorial pieces have been widely quoted, reprinted, and disseminated. Through the feature *Cedars of Lebanon,* it has unearthed and given appealing presentation to neglected or lost masterpieces of Jewish thought and aspiration. By translation or critical discussion, it has brought to the attention of American Jews significant European and Israeli personalities and turns of thought of Jewish relevance. And while, as is the case with any magazine, it runs uneven in quality, article to article, and issue to issue, there is scarcely a number which does not contain something, and often many things, deeply rewarding.

Given all this, what is my complaint against *Commentary?* My complaint is against the spirit which animates it as disclosed in three circumstances: that the magazine has studiously ignored some of the most significant elements in Jewish life; that it has consistently given distorted presentation to certain others, no less crucial; and, finally, that all too frequently it takes on an air of condescension and superciliousness toward matters Jewish, including historic Jewish sanctities, and of offensiveness toward Jewish sensibilities.

✦

I say that *Commentary* ignores, but almost totally, many of the institutions, movements, practices, and programs most essential to Judaism as it now is and as it is most likely to be in the future, if it survives at all. And here let me underscore that I am not pleading on behalf of any institutional vested interest, nor asking the magazine to make of itself a special pleader of any sort.

Nevertheless consider the Synagogue. Is it not among the most conspicuous institutions on the present-day American Jewish scene and perhaps the most influential also? What is more, if there is validity to the opinion, widely expressed of late, that only as a religious communion can Judaism endure in this land, the Synagogue is destined to be the focus of whatever Jewish life is to come.

How then is it possible for any magazine, supposedly concerned with Judaism, to ignore the Synagogue, its structure, its problems and programs, its partisan movements, its potentialities and deficiencies?

Commentary has managed to do just that. In the more than five years of its publication, it has published, to the best of my recollection, scarcely an article on the American Synagogue. But I do not wish to rely on impressions. On this point, as on the others which follow, I have reviewed the files of *Commentary* in detail for the year 1948. One year out of five seems to me to constitute a fair sampling. What is more, the file for 1948 is the latest to be completed, thus representing the magazine at its maturest. Now in the year 1948 *Commentary* averaged eight feature articles per issue, special departments apart, making a total of somewhat under a hundred articles. Of all this total—to revert to the issue at hand—one and only one concerned itself with the Synagogue in any of its phases, and that—I adduce the fact without comment—was from the hand of an ex-chaplain and on the theme: *Why I Gave Up My Congregation.*

Or consider the problem of Jewish observance. For very many Jews this is a burning matter. Most students of Jewish life are agreed that it cannot survive without some regimen of ritual practice. The issue seems not to exist for *Commentary,* which in 1948 gave it not a single article.

As with the Synagogue and Jewish observances, so also with the federations of Synagogues, rabbinical associations, the seminaries which prepare men for the American rabbinate, the American rabbinate as a profession. All smothered in an unbroken blanket of silence.

Or to leave the Synagogue for an area of decision in Judaism no less determinative than it: Jewish education. What is *Commentary's* record on this theme? Throughout 1948, not a single article on the subject in any of its many aspects.

But this is still not the whole story. Is not the Jewish Community Center a characteristic expression of American Jewry, a conspicuous element in its landscape, of profound influence on its future? To the Center, its philosophies, programs and problems, to the Jewish Welfare Board, the nation-wide co-ordinating agency of community centers, to its philosophy, programs and problems, *Commentary* assigned not an article in 1948.

Is the organization of the local Jewish Community, its Federation, its Welfare Fund, its Community Council a matter of consequence to American Jews? Not by *Com-*

mentary's testimony, which in our sample year, did not publish so much as one article concerning it.

Certainly Jewish social work, the problems of preparation and training for it, its ideological issues and conflicting programs, the vexatious riddle of the role of Jewish values in its practice, surely all these ought to engage the earnest attention of a magazine of Jewish interest. *Commentary* in 1948 passed it over in total silence.

There is no end to the themes of Jewish urgency which *Commentary* has let lie fallow: the struggle now in process over national philanthropic budgets; the rebellion of smaller communities against big city and big organization domination; the functioning of the NCRAC, the coordinating instrument for defense agencies, and so on ad libitum.

But these are not only conspicuous issues; on them Jewish survival hangs. Yet these are just the issues *Commentary* has somehow contrived to overlook.

Now perhaps we can account for the air of dilettantism and literary dandyism which hovers over *Commentary,* the impression it lends of being so very much in "the high esthetic line." What is wrong in this respect is not that *Commentary* concerns itself with problems of the creation and criticism of Jewish literature, real issues and deserving of concern, but that it fails so generally to concern itself with the issues of Jewish life.

Most recently (this occurred, however, in 1949 rather than in my test year 1948) *Commentary* ran a two-issue symposium by some twenty contributors on the scarcely urgent question whether Jewish writers find themselves affected in their work by the presence in the Anglo-American literary tradition of anti-Semitic motifs. To such recondite problems, twenty essays, but not even twenty lines to most of the pressing matters I have enumerated and many more that I have left unlisted for lack of time.

No wonder then that the magazine seems ivory towerish and irresponsible, yes, to persons who take Judaism and Jewish life seriously, even trivial.

As with subject matter, so also with contributors. One would expect a Jewish magazine to draw freely, extensively, on the rabbinate, on members of faculties of institutions of Jewish higher learning, on Jewish educators, social workers, communal leaders. After all, these are the groups most expert in Jewish thought and experience. These are the men whose regard for Judaism has led them to make it their life careers.

The absence of just these groups from the roster of *Commentary's* writers is flagrant. Of 1948's articles, one was by the ex-rabbi to whom reference has already been made, a second by another rabbi who has also given up the rabbinate, and only one, one out of almost a hundred, by a rabbi who had enough faith in Judaism and his profession to remain in it. Only one was by a member of the faculty of a Jewish institution of higher learning. None was by a Jewish educator, whether an educator of the top flight like Dushkin, Bergson, Chipkin, or Eisenberg, or by any of their younger colleagues. Indeed, the list of those who have not appeared in *Commentary's* columns would coincide pretty closely with the names which would occur in a Who's Who in American Jewish religious and cultural life.

But these are not only the people who know Judaism best; they are also the leaders of Jewish survivalist effort, of the struggle to assure the continuance of the Jewish enterprise on the American scene. Which means in effect that *Commentary*, a magazine of Jewish interest, is stifling just the groups most devoted to Jewish interests.

There is reason to believe further that this lockout on *Commentary's* part against the persons who represent positive Jewish attitudes carries over into the field of literature itself. The magazine during 1948 overlooked, surprisingly, almost all the distinguished writers part of whose distinction is their Jewish affirmations: Ludwig Lewisohn, for example, Marvin Lowenthal, Marie Syrkin, Maurice Samuel (except for advance chapters from his book on Peretz), Chaim Greenberg, and Irving Fineman.

Perhaps, however, the fault lies not with *Commentary* but with these groups. Perhaps they do not volunteer articles. Plausible at first glance such an explanation dissolves under scrutiny. Anybody conversant with the workings of an editorial office knows that few articles come altogether unsolicited. Indeed, this is the prime business of an editor: to be an entrepreneur, to think of themes and suggest them to likely authors. Which is exactly what the editors of *Commentary* have consistently failed to do with the most informed, committed, and ardent elements of American Jewry.

Or perhaps these people lack writing ability or else opinions worth publishing?

In some instances this may be the case. The possession of a rabbinical diploma, a passion for, or expertness in, Jewish education, leadership in even the greatest Jewish endeavors, constitutes no automatic assurance of literary capability. But granted this, is it not also the function of an editor to recast into intelligibility and grace the ideas of thoughtful but inarticulate people? Besides, while a lack of literary skill may be argued against some, perhaps even many, of American Jewry's educators and rabbis, it is by no means so general, let alone so universal, as the magazine's performance would indicate. Witness the fact that many of them have had books published by leading houses and articles by America's most distinguished journals.

Or perhaps these people have been asked to write for *Commentary* and have refused. But this only deepens the mystery. Is it possible that so heterogeneous a group shall refuse *so* consistently? No other Jewish magazine experiences such a response. Besides, is not *Commentary* a magazine of prestige, is it not virtually the only magazine in American Jewish life which pays its contributors?

Whereupon an interesting question suggests itself. Who are the authors who contribute to *Commentary?* They are of course a widely variegated group and, needless to say, included among them are writers of pronounced Jewish commitments. But the type that recurs most frequently and which therefore comes close to a norm is a young man who has contributed short stories and articles to the publications of the non-Stalinist left.

Now this fact argues nothing against their character or literary abilities and, in my view, pleads much for their social idealism. What makes the point relevant to our purposes is that the entire following of these left publications, writers and readers alike, is marked at best by indifference to Judaism and its survival and more usually by active hostility.

Which leads to a fantastic paradox: there are very many Jews of positive orientation toward Judaism, possessed of significant opinions concerning it, and also of literary skills, who have never been invited to write for *Commentary*. Yet, the American Council for Judaism apart, there is scarcely a Jew negative in attitude toward Jewish values whom the magazine has overlooked as a contributor. And I know of at least two instances of individuals, pronouncedly hostile to Judaism, who have had to resist the importunities of the editors, and this despite open confession of the negativism of their outlook.

So much for what *Commentary* ignores by way of themes and writers. Now for the distortions I allege against it.

Consider that issue, until recently the most controversial of all Jewish issues: political Zionism. On the reportorial level, so far as concerns descriptions of events in Israel, the United Nations and among the D.P.'s the magazine has done a good job of providing honest, objective coverage. But so soon as ideology and policy are at stake, the presentation has been not only biased but deviously so.

This is the record for 1948. I count a total of sixteen articles on Palestine and Zionism. Of these, eight are purely or almost purely reportorial, that is to say, they record and interpret events with little or no attempt to suggest policies either to Israelis or American Jews. Eight remain then as dealing with policy.

Of these, no less than six, or three quarters, are non-Zionist, ranging from outright anti-Zionism to such borderline Zionist positions as Ihud. Only two reflect mainline Zionist thought. If ever there was an instance of an unrepresentative coverage of a controversial issue, this is it.

As with Zionism, so also with theology. Here too *Commentary,* when it does not engage in outright attack, as it did in the very first article it published on the theme, a beautifully written statement of philosophical atheism, distorts the picture by overemphasizing fringe positions. Prevailingly, when it interprets or evaluates Judaism as a system of affirmations, it does so in terms of Kierkegaard or the neo-Reformationist outlook, legitimate enough as a coign of vantage, but scarcely either the most significant, let alone the sole, touchstone. Most important and revealing is the temper with which *Commentary* takes recourse to the existentialist and crisis theology. It uses them less as a source of possible enrichment of the Jewish religion than as a stick with which to beat it, an occasion for pouring contempt on Judaism, the Synagogue, and the rabbinate alike.

As with Zionism and theology, so also with Reconstructionism, which quite obviously is not to the liking of *Commentary's* editors. The magazine made its bow to the world in a first issue containing an account of Reconstructionism so distorted that I who have been associated with the movement since its very beginning and have been taken by Dr. Kaplan, its founder, to be a faithful expositor of it, did not recognize the cause with which I was identified. To be sure, thereafter an opportunity for response was made available to Dr. Kaplan. But as is so generally the case with defenses and retractions, the damage may well have been beyond retrieving. In any event, Reconstructionism has ever after had short shrift and rough treatment at *Commentary*'s hands.

I turn now to the third and last of the items in my bill of particulars. It was William Paley, the English divine, who once asked: "Who can refute a sneer?" To which a more troublesome question must be appended: how is one to prove that a sneer is intended? For he whom we charge with sneering can always protest: "But I am only smiling" or else, "These are the natural lineaments of my face."

I cannot therefore establish my next point incontrovertibly as I could in the case of *Commentary*'s omissions, nor presumably as with *Commentary*'s distortions. Nevertheless I assert concerning *Commentary* that though it does not always sneer at Judaism and Jewish life in America it does so often enough to make the expression fairly typical of the cast of its countenance.

Every person I have talked to on the matter is persuaded of the presence of a sneer in *The Month in History*, a regular department of the magazine issue until October, 1948. Written in its earlier days by Mr. Sidney Hertzberg, the feature professed to be a review of the month's events of Jewish interest. Now the appearance of this department coincided with the period when the full horror of the concentration camps and gas chambers was being disclosed, when the tragedy of the D.P.'s was emerging into light of day, when the Labor Party was busy breaking Britain's word to the Jews and Bevin acted and spoke in an anti-Semitic manner—all this culminating in the monstrosity of the deportation back to Germany of the passengers of the S.S. Exodus 1947. It was a time when every sensitive Jew, every sensitive human being, wondered at times that he was not going mad with grief and outrage. But not the writer of *The Month in History*.

To him, the Zionist attempt to open the doors of Palestine appeared not as an expression of rightous indignation nor an insistence on mercy for the D.P.'s but as merely a "pressure campaign." The rejection of the Anglo-American Commission on Palestine of a Jewish State seemed to please Mr. Hertzberg. In him British policy in Palestine found an apologist: "If Soviet influence was to be kept out of the Middle East and if Anglo-American routes and resources were to be protected, the first job of the two powers was to insure a *modus vivendi* with Arab leaders."

Worse than what this columnist said was the manner in which he said it. In the presence of one of the most tragic ordeals in all history, he remained unmoved, aloof, superior to it all, his manner as he watched the anguished contortions of Jews suggested nothing so much as an entomologist studying, with no feeling except distaste, the antics of some remote and peculiarly ugly insect.

Many of us have felt too that sneers lurk in not a few of the essays descriptive of American Jewish life and published under the caption *From the American Scene*. And not rabbis and other professional Jews alone. At least one of the writers for *Commentary*, a contributor several times over to this very department, a young woman of warm and positive Jewish attachments, has told me that such is the mood of the magazine and its influence on her that whenever she undertakes an assignment for it she finds herself writing with an altogether uncharacteristic condescension toward Jewish values and practices.

The recently published piece by Isaac Rosenfeld entitled *Adam and Eve on Delancey Street* has already been discussed adequately and more. I have no desire to discuss, let alone to denounce it further. If I refer to it, it is only because it bears out so strongly the point I am making. There is no explaining the publication of that unfortunate essay by the editors of *Commentary,* nor of the grudging nature of their subsequent apology, except in the assumption of an inadequate respect on their part toward Jews and the Jewish tradition.

This is my bill of particulars. Given it, what is the answer to the question whether *Commentary* is more a benefit or a detriment to Jewish life? There is of course no way of answering such a question with definitiveness. The matter being one of immeasurables and imponderables, neither alternative can be established with anything approaching finality. This much, however, is sure, that whatever the good *Commentary* is effecting, it is working harm also.

The air it assumes toward Judaism and Jews is scarcely conducive to heightening Jewish ardor or self-esteem. The distortions, as is the way with distortions, are misleading and therefore dangerous. The silence of the magazine on urgent issues of Jewish living—the Synagogue, observance, community organization, and the rest—tends to withhold from the consideration of Jews matters of grave concern to them. Or, if they retain a recollection of these matters, they are likely, under *Commentary's* influence, to minimize their gravity. Obviously were these issues as serious as they had supposed, they would not have been so studiously ignored by a responsible publication. Rabbis and educators by indirection are made to appear incapable of writing acceptable prose or devoid of ideas worth putting into print, else *Commentary* would be publishing them. And since it is largely negative Jews who do get into *Commentary's* pages, the impression is fostered of a Jewish negativism within American Jewry, indeed a nihilism, greater than it is in fact, which is great enough. Thereby, escapist Jews are encouraged in their escapism and loyalist Jews disheartened, and *Commentary* becomes guilty of violating the injunction that one should never throw a stone after a man who is already falling.

In the light of the foregoing, one other issue comes into doubt, whether *Commentary* is fulfilling the terms of the agreement whereunder it receives monies that stem ultimately from the U.J.A.* I have never been certain in my own mind of the propriety of this arrangement. The publication of a magazine like *Commentary* is not a purpose which most U.J.A. donors have in mind when they make their pledges, nor does the U.J.A. promotional material go out of its way to enlighten them in this respect. Nor do I,

---

* This was a fact when written. The arrangement was subsequently changed.

when from my pulpit on Kol Nidre night I appeal on U.J.A.'s behalf. Doubtful about this procedure, I make no issue of it. U.J.A. leaders, better versed in fund raising than I, say that the gain to U.J.A. through the elimination of competitive drives outweighs the cost, and I am prepared to take their word.

But the money is not just given to *Commentary* by U.J.A. in fee simple. There is supposed to be a return, a *quid pro quo,* on *Commentary's* part. The understanding is that the magazine is rendering service as an instrument of Jewish self-defense against anti-Semitism.

It is just this assumption which seems questionable to me.

Are Jews likely to be more steadfast against their enemies after being exposed to the negative aspects of *Commentary?* Are they not likely rather to be disheartened, to feel a sense of pointlessness and futility about the entire Jewish effort?

Or is it Christians whose respect for Jews *Commentary* is supposed to awaken and intensify? Such would seem to be the thesis of *Commentary's* promotional material. But over this I am particularly disquieted. I am not one who worries excessively about what Gentiles think of Jews and Judaism. My concern is more with what Jews think of it and themselves. Nevertheless, I am not sure of the effect of *Commentary* on Gentiles, especially Gentiles of spirituality and sensibility.

What are non-Jews likely to think of us, how can they regard us with respect, after the spectacles of Jewish cynicism, irreligion, spiritual vacuity, and self-contempt which this magazine stages from time to time?

One last question remains: How are we to account for everything we have considered, most especially, the paradox of a Jewish magazine so broadly negative to Jewish interests and values?

A hypothesis offers itself.

It can be argued that editors of *Commentary* afford but an unusually self-revelatory instance of a phenomenon too common to require detailed description: the rootless Jewish intellectual; the Jew alienated from, yet drawn to, the Jewish faith, tradition, and people; ambivalent toward them, that is to say, loving and hating them at the same time; indeed simultaneously approving and despising his own personality for its irretrievable Jewishness.

A large plausibility invests this hypothesis. It would account for the presence of these men in Jewish letters, when each of them, without overly serious difficulty, could find a livelihood somewhere in the larger literary world. It would account for the warmth which the magazine so often displays toward the Jewish past and Jewish life at a distance, where it does not come too close to the editors or touch them too intimately. It would account, in a word, for all the positive aspects of *Commentary* over and above the technical. These would be the love side of the ambivalence.

But it would account equally for the negative features, the suppression or distortion of all those elements in American Jewish life, the Jewishness—be it noted—near at hand, which are survivalist in import, for the superciliousness and contemptfulness, which are really self-contempt. In these the *sitra abra,* the other darker force in the polarity, is asserting itself.

If this is so, then I cannot refrain from remarking that a grave dereliction of duty must be charged against the duly constituted officials of the American Jewish Committee. Launching a magazine of Jewish reference they made sure of the technical competence in its editors but not of their Jewish temper. Which is an act of negligence akin to that of a mother who turns over her child to the care of a nurse possessed of all qualifications except an affection for children.

But all this is water over the dam. The issue now, given this publication as it is, is the comparative strength of Jewish love and hate in the editors as a group and as individuals.

Should *Commentary* persist in its course to the present, slighting positive elements in Jewish life, or distorting them, or sneering at them, and this despite the mounting chorus of protest, in which this is but one voice, then we shall have no alternative except to assume that the hate is incorrigible, that the publication therefore is regrettably the enemy of our souls as Jews. We shall then have no choice except to do it battle with all the force at our disposal.

Nor ought we to be overly patient in our insistence on visible evidences that it is the love of Judaism and not the hate which is the stronger. *Commentary* and its editors

have by now had five years of public forbearance and sub-
sidy, a half decade, in which to wander out of their Jewish wastelands, if not into, then at least in the direction of,
a promised land. If there is in this magazine and its editors
the possibility of dedication to Judaism, then we have the
right to expect some signs of it, "speedily, soon and in our
days."

On the other hand, we must not prejudge the outcome
at all, certainly not adversely, unless we have to, and until
we have exhausted every moral influence at our disposal.

We must call to the attention of the editors of *Commentary,* as I am attempting to do in this paper, their
lapses and errors. We must reprove their negativisms can-
didly. At the same time we must encourage every tendency
on their part to Jewish affirmation.

The attitude we ought to take toward the editors of
Commentary is caught in one episode, and that authorita-
tive with antiquity.

It is related of Rabbi Jochanan bar Napcha that once he
encountered Simeon son of Lakish, destined to become a
great sage in Israel, but in those days a gladiator, alienated
from, hostile to, contemptuous of, Jewish morality and
learning. We know that Simeon taunted Rabbi Jochanan
to provoke him. Jochanan refused to be angered. Instead
he said to him only this, but it sufficed: "Your strength
would well befit the Torah."

Such must be our plea to the editors of *Commentary,*
communicated by every open channel:

Your talents would well befit the Torah.

Recommendations *

A. WRITERS

I should like to suggest to *Commentary* a systematic exploitation of *all* the writer resources of the American Jewish community, *including its normative elements,* that is to say, rabbis, educators, social workers, communal leaders, research scholars, etc. (For a technique of procedure, see below.) These are much richer than may have been recognized by the Editorial Board; certainly far richer than the columns of the magazine suggest.

In addition to persons capable of expressing themselves acceptably, there are sizable groups possessed of special knowledge and experience with whom *Commentary* should work along the lines suggested to the editors by Dr. Louis Finkelstein. It is his recommendation that writers be assigned to academicians and laymen alike who have something of Jewish consequence to say but lack either the energy or skill to say it passably. Jewish scholarship is one such field, social work at home and abroad another; the Yiddish writing world, especially *YIVO,* a third; the lay leadership of the American Jewish community is still a fourth.

To this end, it will be necessary for the editors of *Commentary* to overcome the antagonism with which it is widely regarded in just these circles. Patience, perseverance, the high magnetism of the publication as a literary platform, and, above all, a repeated, visible demonstration

* Written in March 1950 and published posthumously.

of respect on its part for the life-interests and sanctities of these groups should prevail in the end.

A parenthesis on rabbis as potential contributors to Commentary:

It has been suggested by some members of the Publications Committee, in defense of *Commentary's* failure to publish rabbis more frequently, (a) that no more than a half dozen rabbis are capable of writing for the publication and (b) that the editors have freely invited rabbis to contribute only to be refused.

The notion that literate and thoughtful rabbis are so few is a slander. Here is a random list, which could be extended widely, of some rabbis of demonstrated ability as authors on Jewish themes, either unpublished or seriously under-published by *Commentary:* Jacob Agus, Bernard Bamberger, Philip Bernstein, Samuel Blumenfield, Ben Zion Bokser, Mortimer Cohen, Abraham Cronbach, Ira Eisenstein, Solomon Freehof, Roland Gittelson, Nelson Glueck, Judah Goldin, Solomon Goldman, Robert Gordis, Leo Jung, Mordecai Kaplan, Eugene Kohn, Felix Levy, Theodore Lewis, Jacob Marcus, Joseph Narot, David Polish, David de Sola Pool, Joshua Trachtenberg, Jacob Weinstein.

This is a far from exhaustive enumeration, and it does not begin to reckon with the many unpublished men in the rabbinate (as in other fields of Jewish interest) whom the editors of *Commentary* are under an obligation to draw out.

Have these rabbis been invited to write?
Many not at all!

158

Some only to comment on articles by one or the other of the editors, which to a person interested in primary writing of his own, constitutes a scant and grudging invitation indeed.

Even these as a rule only tardily and after the magazine had been operating long enough to engender the hostility in which it is now held, so that the typical rabbi's impulse is to have no traffic with *Commentary* on any terms.

This much is certain: the rabbinate as a whole is convinced, and with warrant, of hostility toward itself on the part of *Commentary's* editors. This is a sentiment that requires overcoming.

B. THEMES

In my lecture of November 18th I listed large fields of Jewish concern neglected by *Commentary:* among others, the Synagogue, observance, Jewish education, the community center, communal structure, social work, etc.

Each of these areas—and others can be added—is itself a nest of subordinate themes of great Jewish pertinence.

The following are random examples of topics, some falling within the categories just mentioned, others not, but in any case not to be overlooked by a Jewish publication alert to the world which it expresses and to which it addresses itself.

1. *The rise of veterans' Synagogues,* how far it is spontaneous, how far contrived; how much a matter of religion, how much of sociality.

2. *Conversions to Judaism,* of which the number is considerable and by no means all for motives of marriage.

3. *Apostasies from Judaism,* a fascinating theme, embracing as it does such personalities as the late Professor Emanuel Chapman of Fordham and Hunter Colleges and the personalities mentioned by Merton in his *Seven Storey Mountain.*

4. *Intermarriage,* the statistics, the changing orientation of the Jewish community.

5. *The rise of the Jewish Day School.*

6. *The worth of the National Conference of Christians and Jews,* and, for that matter, of the civic defense programs of the Anti Defamation League, the American Jewish Committee, the Committee on Law and Social Action of the American Jewish Congress.

7. *The sociology of smaller Jewish communities,* the theme of such a book as Albert Gordon's *Jews in Transition* and of the series now in process in *The National Jewish Post.*

8. *The status of kashruth.*

9. *The crisis in Conservative Judaism over issues of ritual,* an issue threatening the continued unity of Conservative Judaism.

10. *Problems of Jewish Law* and its adaptation to contemporary life, indeed basic expositions of the fundamentals of Jewish law, on which theme a variety of experts is available.

11. *The Janowsky report,* a critique and an appraisal of its implementation by the National Jewish Welfare

Board and the Community Centers which formally rati-
fied it.

12. *New developments in Jewish scholarship*, the Su-
koenig-Zeitlin controversy, for example.

To persist in neglecting themes of this order is not only
to commit a disservice to Jewish life, it is to be guilty of
unresourceful journalism.

But no less important than the broadening of the scope
of *Commentary* is the rectification of its emotional imbal-
ance. The fault found with the publication is not alone
that its themes have been arbitrarily limited but that
those taken up have been prejudicially treated and animated by contempt for the Jewish tradition. There will,
of course, be matters on which the editors and readers
will desire partisan or critical presentations. But when a
disinterested discussion is indicated, let it be truly disinterested and not a partisanship masquerading as neutrality.
Beyond all else let the spirit always be, even in criticisms
of Judaism, an ultimate love and reverence.

C. A SUGGESTION AS TO PROCEDURE

The controversy over *Commentary* reduces itself finally
to an either-or. Either the editors of *Commentary* have
all along been unaware of the many possible themes and
authors of positive Jewish import (A and B, this section)
or, aware of them, have out of bias denied them a hear-
ing.

If the second alternative prevail, they have no business
acting as editors of a publication of Jewish reference nor

has the American Jewish Committee, as a custodian of communal interests and funds, the right to retain them in their posts.

Under the former alternative, which is both more charitable and hopeful, the editors of *Commentary* are of good will but inadequate knowledge. And indeed so complex and variegated has Jewish life become that any individual or group, no matter how earnest and well informed, must be inexpert in some direction.

To rectify any such inescapable deficiency, a panel of consultants should be established comprising one or more authorities in all fields of Jewish interest: scholarship, organized religion in its various denominations, theologies and ideologies, education, social work, community organization after its many species, art, music, Hebrew literature, Yiddish literature, demography, Jewries abroad, etc., etc.

It would be the function of these consultants, whether through formal meetings or by correspondence, to feed the Board of Editors suggestions as to themes of interest and consequence, as to persons qualified to write on them, and also as to potential writers from within these fields who should be drawn forth.

Editorial freedom and responsibility would continue as at present. Literary standards would be unaffected. Yet there would be reasonable hope of an end to the omissions and biased presentations which have distorted *Commentary* heretofore and prevented it from ministering to the Jewish community as effectively as it might.

D. A FINAL WORD

The end of the matter, all things having been heard: the editors of *Commentary* owe no accounting to any single individual, let alone to the writer of this memorandum. But they do owe reassurance to the Jewish community which supports their enterprise to whose welfare they are professedly committed. Such reassurance may take whatever shape the editors desire. It need not, indeed it should not, be in the form of any retraction or confession of error. Yet somehow the editors of *Commentary* need to inform the Jewish public that they will in the future cover the Jewish scene more representatively, fairly, and creatively than in the past, and with heightened respect and solicitude for historic Jewish purposes and sanctities.

Whatever form it take, such reassurance will be recognized, and gratefully. Failing it, this correspondent and others of like mind with him will regard themselves as free to do whatever in their judgment Jewish interests require.

An Apology and Retraction

In my address I put the rhetorical question: "What shall one make of a Jewish magazine which, to the present day, almost two years after its appearance, has yet to publish a review of so consequential a work by so consequential an author as *The Future of the American Jew* by Mordecai Kaplan?"

A member of the Publications Committee had chided me: "Did you take the trouble to find the reason why?"

The fact is that I did. I addressed inquiries on this

score, not to the editors of *Commentary,* to be sure, to whom I did not feel free to turn, but to the Reconstructionist Foundation.

A spokesman for the Foundation informed me that one of its officers, exercised as I was, had addressed an inquiry to the office of *Commentary.* He had been informed that the review had in fact been assigned to a reviewer of high distinction who had however first lost his copy of the book and then become too involved in editing a work of his own to attend to the assignment promptly.

The spokesman for the Foundation who relayed this explanation did so indignantly and incredulously, pointing out that it does not take forever to replace the lost copy of a book which is very much in print and, further, that it is not uncommon for editors to reassign reviews when an original reviewer cannot discharge his obligation with reasonable promptitude.

Sharing my informant's conviction of the inadequacy of the explanation, I asked the question at issue with an altogether clear conscience.

Nevertheless, in a letter dated November 25th, Dr. Kaplan wrote to me: "I feel however that I should acquaint you with the facts concerning the proposed review of my book. . . . Therefore, in this instance, *Commentary* itself is not at fault."

The facts I already possessed. What was crucial in Dr. Kaplan's letter was that he regarded them as constituting a satisfactory explanation.

For having been more zealous on my master's behalf

than he himself feels to have been warranted, for having, like the person who relayed the explanation to me, been of "little faith" concerning it, and, most of all, for not having judged the editors of *Commentary* in "the scale of merit" on this point, I owe them an apology which I tender herewith.

CHAPTER 10

THE TEST OF TIME *

(On the Fifteenth Anniversary of *The Reconstructionist*)

☀☀☀☀☀☀☀☀☀☀☀☀☀☀☀☀☀☀☀☀☀☀☀☀☀☀☀☀☀

To be confronted with old expressions of one's opinions is not always a pleasurable experience; on occasion it can be acutely embarrassing. The matters over which one once waxed hot too often appear in perspective quite inconsequential. Axioms may have become moot, sure-fire procedures may have fizzled. Blessed is he in doctrine, purpose, and feeling, whose latter time, to paraphrase the ancient rabbis, is not shamed by his former.

The fifteenth anniversary at hand of the founding of *The Reconstructionist* magazine and movement, I set myself recently to looking backward to their beginnings as preserved in *The Reconstructionist Papers,* a compilation of the first year's articles and editorials. That much has been amiss with Reconstructionism is evident from the state of Jewish life to the regeneration of which the

* Written in February, 1950 and published in *The Reconstructionist* magazine.

movement has been dedicated all along. That of that much some at least was present at birth is apparent to the wisdom of hindsight. What is more, over and above innate deficiencies in the basic and original conception there have been many in execution, failures not of the idea but on the part of the men who propound it. Yet, with all this freely admitted, the bulk of Reconstructionism, theory, program, implementation, seems to me to stand up under the test of the years and indeed to have been validated by it. Before us, then, is an instance, not too frequent in human affairs, of a latter time which not only need not be shamed by the former but which has reason, modest and restrained, but reason nonetheless, to take pride in it and, taking pride, to reaffirm commitments and objectivity.

II

At core and in essence, Reconstructionism is a definition. It declares Judaism to be the evolving religious civilization of the Jewish people.

In this formula, every word counts both as a negation and an affirmation. "Evolving" denies the static Judaism of neo-Orthodoxy and insists on the unremitting legitimacy and desirability of the new in Jewish affairs. "Religious" rejects the secularisms of race, nationalism, culture and, on an unreflective level, of mindless, purposeless, Torahless and Godless Jewish sociality. Contrariwise it requires some form of theistic commitment as a central element in Jewish living. "Civilization" repudiates the truncated Judaism of old-line Reform and also of contemporary Jewish escapists, which, by limiting Jewishness to faith alone, hopes to make it slight in scope and significance. At the same time, it demands the nurturing of all the variegated aspects of Jewish experience and aspiration. Finally, "Jewish people" breaks the procrusteanism which allows only one form for Jewish group life, affirming against it the possibility of diversity within each setting and also setting to setting—nationhood in Israel, for example, and a religio-cultural character in America, a cultural attachment for one American Jew, religious for a second—and yet insisting simultaneously on a unity and reciprocity among Jews and Jewries more fundamental than theological formulations, cultural differences, or social and political status.

This definition has been revealed by the passing of a decade and a half as valid and creative. It has not only not been disproved by any event or turn of thought which the years have cast up, but has showed itself capable of growth—as one test of the vitality of a conception—and—a second and necessary criterion of the soundness of any hypothesis—has proved itself capable of accounting for new phenomena as they have arisen.

Increasingly validated by events, the theory of Reconstructionism has never been permitted to freeze into a fixity. Patiently, painstakingly, it has been worked through again and again to take cognizance of the new in thought and situation. Not the least of the virtues of the ideology as such has been its ability to "cover" such novelties. And because, basically adequate to begin with, it has been under continuous testing, refinement, and adaptation, it is the only theory of Jewish life not caught off base by re-

168

cent revolutionary events. Here is one philosophy which is not bewildered by the simultaneous presence of a Jewish nation in Israel and a Jewish religio-cultural fellowship in America, which, unlike secular Zionism, is stimulated rather than bankrupted by the realization of one of the greatest of historic Jewish purposes, which understands now, because it figured it out long ago, how and in what fashion an American Jew can be attached to Israel and yet be both a complete American and a full Jew in his own right and in no fashion, a "colonial" of Israel.

If only as a matter of esthetics, there is something exciting about the intellectual adequacy of the Reconstructionist schematism. Actually, the Kaplanian formulation has been taken up, in whole or in part, openly or covertly, by a variety of Jewish organizations and movements. It is *the* philosophy of Conservative Judaism, so far as Conservative Judaism has any at all. Its imprint is clear and deep on the new "Columbus" platform of Reform. It underlies the Janowsky report, now the officially authorized blueprint of the National Jewish Welfare Board and of its constituent Community Centers. And, in another direction, it is among the goads prodding Jewish secularists to a rapport with the Jewish religion.

III

As with theory, so with ritual usage. The broad outlines of the Reconstructionist position were drawn in *Judaism as a Civilization:* the conception of observance as *minhag* (folkway), rather than *din* (law), and yet folkway as integral and indispensable to Jewish life; the demand for directed change attended by a simultaneous insistence on tradition.

Matured fifteen years ago, the Kaplanian position has undergone development since a process culminating in the publication in 1941 of *Toward a Guide for Jewish Ritual Usage*. In this brochure general principles were brought down to cases. Criteria were established for the adjustment of the conflicting demands of the traditional and the contemporary. Sketches were made, tentative but precise, of the shape of several key, sensitive areas of Jewish practice under revision according to plan.

Over and above the utility of all this in aiding individuals to a solution of their private problems, Reconstructionism has exerted considerable influence on institutional and organizational positions. Its argument for the necessity of ritual usage, its nonrevelationist, nonhalakhic ideology of observance, have been contributants to Reform's reversal in mindset and program on the issue.

Within Conservative Judaism, the record of achievement has been mixed, which is startling and perhaps ominous, in view of the fact that here, so to speak, is Reconstructionism's back yard and special preserve. Efficiency, like charity, ought to begin at home. On the one hand, Kaplanism has been the chief theorizer, prod, and rallying point for the forces pressing for official, orderly, candid revisions in practice. On the other hand, tangible and determinable results have been negligible. Despite the fact that Reconstructionism has on its side, in the tug of war that has so long racked Conservative Judaism, greater forthrightness, the more cogent argument, the demon-

strated needs and preferences of Conservative Jews and synagogues, even a heavy superiority in man power, lay and
rabbinical, it cannot point to so much as a skirmish de-
cisively won against its "rightist" opposition.

This performance, or more aptly absence of performance, seems to me in the first instance a consequence of
personal inadequacies. The leaders of Reconstructionism
may be right in theory; they have been consistently out-
maneuvered, tactically, so totally indeed that to the present not a single issue of the revision of observance has so
much as been brought to a head, to the point where men
are called upon to declare "aye" or "nay." As Fabius
Cunctator established, to prevent a battle from being
joined is already a victory for the weaker as against the
stronger force.

But an explanation in terms of personalities is too easy
and too superficial. Deeper and less obvious factors are involved, which, surprisingly enough in the case of a cause
committed to logical lucidity, are themselves ideological in
character. Reconstructionism, so clear about Judaism in the
large, is quite turgid in its thinking about itself and the
organizational entities with which it deals. It has, for example, never succeeded in making up its mind on the nature of Conservative Judaism, whether indeed any such
entity exists which is more than an adventitious alliance
of synagogues too traditional to be Reform but not traditional enough to be Orthodox. This irresolution, incidentally, is not of Reconstructionist creation. It pervades all
Conservatism and is largest where it should be least, in
the Seminary and its faculty. Be that as it may, the fact

remains that the Reconstructionist high command, not quite certain as to what it is dealing with when it addresses itself to Conservative Judaism, deals with it unsteadily.

Far more debilitating to Reconstructionism, *both vis à vis* Conservative Judaism and Jewry at large, has been its indecision concerning itself. From the very inception it halted between the two opinions: "School of Thought" and "Movement," plumping in the end for the former, but with frequent and intense *arrières pensées* after the latter.

A good case can be made for the thesis that Reconstructionism at the very start should have declared itself a movement in its own name and right. For its failure to do so it has suffered the disability of being identified with a particular wing of American Jewry without a compensating influence over it and its organizational apparatus. It has been restrained in its freedom, not of thought to be sure, but of action. And it has never raised a standard of its own to which individuals and institutions, sympathetic to its principles, might repair and, by assemblng and working together for these principles, lend them greater actuality. Why then was the step not taken? Timidity played a part, I suspect, but even more institutional loyalties, the reluctance to fragmentize an already splintered Jewish life, and most of all, the failure to think through the nature of Reconstructionism.

The issue now is largely academic. The time to launch a movement is when its ideology is first enunciated, when under its initial impact men are ready to sever old associations and undertake new ones on its behalf, before they come to take it for granted and, having had the experience of simultaneous loyalty to it and an older allegiance, to prefer the comfort of abiding, even if unquietly, with both.

If the prospect of Reconstructionism's becoming a movement persists at all to the present, it is because of the impasse as to ideology and law within Conservative Judaism. Pressures for authorized revisions in both fields have mounted steadily, but have as steadily been resisted. Conservative Judaism then presents the classic picture of the immovable object and the irresistible force, and so long as that is the case, the possibility of an eventual explosion and consequent organizational realignment cannot be ruled out.

IV

In no field has the Reconstructionist reading of the American Jewish scene proved more accurate than in community organization. Both deductively, as an inference from its definition of Judaism, and inductively, as a generalization based on keen perceptions of the actualities of Jewish life, Dr. Kaplan had early projected the Community Council as the most promising pattern for the local community and the only reliable base for a nation-wide organization. The events of the last fifteen years have vindicated this judgment.

Community Councils have grown apace. They have proved capable of efficiency, democracy, creativity. The organization of American Jewry "from on top" has been demonstrated as wasteful and, in a crisis, undependable.

National agencies continue as of old to jostle for position. They duplicate each other's efforts and, despite all attempts at co-ordination, persist deeply, irremediably competitive. What is more, when under the spur of a vast crisis The American Jewish Conference was convoked, it split asunder on the first major controversial issue with which it was confronted. That the secession of the American Jewish Committee over a pronouncement in favor of a Jewish commonwealth in Palestine has been proved a blunder serves only to render the episode the more pathetic and telling. Quite clearly, organizations accountable only to themselves can never be better than unsteady piers for a bridge uniting the diverse elements of the American Jewish community. Democracy, responsibility to the people, the political hope of mankind, is also, as Reconstructionism long ago declared it, the communal hope of the variegated and voluntaristic fellowship which is American Jewry.

V

In one respect, *The Reconstructionist Papers* of fifteen years ago are misleading. They afford only the scantiest evidence of the division among the editors over theology, already present then, as I can recall, but destined to grow in depth and intensity until it is for many, myself included, the gravest reservation from the prevailing Reconstructionist position.

The Kaplanian outlook is there fully evolved: the definition of God as "the power which endorses what we believe ought to be," a variant of the classic formulation in

174

terms of the forces that make for salvation and the enhancement of life; the resolute setting aside of the metaphysical issues of the divine existence and the cosmological as to the relation between God and the universe. "The God idea," writes Dr. Kaplan, "is not the conception of an entity. . . ." "The God idea," Rabbi Eugene Kohn asserts, "does not function differently if we think of God as a being, or a quality or aspect of reality that sustains and gives worth to human personality."

I have no desire to raise again a controversy which has had extensive airing. Yet, I cannot refrain from reiterating that to me the Kaplan-Kohn position on this score was and remains inadequate. I understand and respect the motives behind it: a conviction of the futility of metaphysical speculation, the desire to retrieve from the historic God-idea its most meaningful, its experimental elements, the hope, confidence, and goodness it has inspired.

For me, however, the riddle of the universe is not so readily to be dismissed, and faith is not only a psychological and ethical venture but a cognitive one also, an affirmation concerning the ultimate nature of things. Nor do I believe, as does Rabbi Kohn, that one can have the benefits of faith in God without a venture as to His existence as an entity.

Dr. Kaplan and the Editorial Board of *The Reconstructionist* have denied vigorously that any particular theology is integral to Reconstructionism. Expressions of other viewpoints have been solicited and published freely. Nevertheless, Reconstructionism is understandably identified with what Dr. Kaplan thinks on this theme as on all others.

The consequence within the Editorial Board has been a cleft which is responsible for the alienation of some, fortunately only a few, of Reconstructionism's otherwise most ardent friends. In the general community this circumstance has also worked adversely. The hard fact is that, for the success of the movement, its ability to rally a following, Dr. Kaplan has been either too much or too little a theologian. Had he been none at all, his sociology of Jewish life would have appealed, purely as a sociology, to secularists and religionists equally. Had he been more, he would have proved a more acceptable rallying point for conventionally religious Jews. As matters stand, he is too theoretical for secularists and not theoretical enough for the traditionally or metaphysically minded.

VI

On one defect of Reconstructionism time has failed to work even the slightest improvement. I refer to the style in which it expresses itself.

Not that that style is without virtue. It is direct, and, for those who will take the time to work over it. lucid. But it is not light or easy, and certainly not beautiful or incendiary. Among those who have taken up the Reconstructionist cause poets and journalists are included, but not, it would seem, among Reconstructionist editors. Or if they are present, their influence over their colleagues is slight or their colorfulness has been muted by the encircling sobriety.

For want of a horse, a shoe, a nail—a kingdom was once lost. Who shall say what American Judaism has lost because this hopeful, creative vision of Jewish living has never found a spokesman of eloquence equal to its possibilities?

Nor can this failure in literary expression have been altogether without effect in working another disappointment. What the other editors expected of Reconstructionism at the time it was first launched I cannot say. But it seems altogether likely that they shared my hope of rousing a revolution, kindling a fire, within American Jewry. Our labors, it can be said soberly, modestly, have not been without effect. We have exerted influences, helped to keep burning in many breasts flames not of our kindling and, on occasion though not often enough, put a torch here to one heart and there another. But we have not started and are unlikely ever to start a general conflagration.

Is the deficiency in us? If so, it is not for want of flame in at least some of our company. In all the world no one feels more constantly and intimately than does Dr. Kaplan the *elbonah shel Torah* (the grievance of the neglected Torah), nor is anyone more passionate and resolute over its ultimate vindication. Is it that American Jewry is no longer inflammable, that the love and loyalty for the Tradition to which Reconstructionism appeals is by now beyond catching fire? Or, more hopefully, perhaps the role of Reconstructionism in the American Jewish future is not that of an Ezra but of the unknown scribes before him who ordered the way of life to which later he rallied his people. Perhaps, in a word, it is not to be expected of analyses and programs, whether Kaplanian or any

177

other, that they shall themselves deliver, it being their function rather to clear the way which deliverance must travel. Perhaps, indeed, the whole notion of an American Jewry finding itself in a sudden blaze, no matter by whom kindled, is too romantic for actuality. There may be no possibility of *kefitzat haderekh* (traversing the road by miraculous leaps and bounds), in the work of redemption, but only a slow, effortful plodding, one step after another.

In any case, the chilling truth stands: "The harvest is past, the summer is ended, and we are not saved." Judaism in America has not yet passed its perils or fulfilled its promises.

Wherefore, the struggle goes on. In it, and regardless of outcome, Reconstructionism, for all its limitations, has been and remains a force of intelligence and candor, affirmation and spirituality, idealism and practicality, of catholicity yet commitment, of realism yet unabated hope.

If defeat is destined, this much has already been established: it shall not have been unresisted, nor the vanquished without honor. If victory is to be the event, it will not be won otherwise than along these lines.

III

ISRAEL

CHAPTER 11

WHEN I THINK OF SERAYE *

I HAVE been thinking a great deal of late about Seraye. What, you will ask, is Seraye?

Seraye is a village situated in the Lithuanian County of Suwalki, just to the east of the old German frontier.

And what—to paraphrase Hamlet—is Seraye to me or I to Seraye?

Seraye, as it chances, is the town whence my family stems, where my father was born, from which he set forth at the ripe age of ten to continue his Talmudic studies at more conspicuous seats of learning—a venture which ended up, after many wanderings, physical and spiritual, in this land.

I say that I have been thinking about Seraye a great deal of late, and for a compelling reason. I cannot think about all of Europe's Jews: the six million dead, the one and a half millions of walking skeletons. Such numbers are too large for me to embrace, the anguish they repre-

---

* An address delivered at the rally of the Women's Division of the United Jewish Appeal held in the Waldorf-Astoria Hotel, New York City.

sent too vast for my comprehension. And so I think of Seraye instead.

Now since, in all likelihood, there is not another person in this auditorium who has even so much as heard of Seraye, I would not have ventured to speak of it, were it not that each of us has a Seraye, some place of origin abroad from which, as the case may be, we or our parents, or grandparents or remote forebears set out for the New World.

These Serayes may lie in Germany or France or England or Hungary or Poland rather than Lithuania; they may be large cities rather than villages. In any event they are places toward which we feel some personal bond, and constitute therefore a handle by which we may the more readily and vividly lay hold of the agony of Europe today and of the even deeper agony of Europe's Jews.

Let me then speak to you of Seraye, and do you, as I speak, translate it into its equivalent in your own lives. So we will make real and concrete for ourselves the largest and most terrible tragedy in all recorded time.

Let me confess here and now that, having been born in America, I have never seen Seraye, let alone set foot in it. And yet I am sure I am well acquainted with it. I know it from the tales told me by my father, from descriptions of similar towns in books like Irving Fineman's *Hear Ye Sons*, and Maurice Samuel's *World of Sholem Aleichem*, from the writings of its inhabitants, and most of all, from the kind of people it produced.

I know for example of Seraye that, though it was a tiny town, it made up in poverty for what it lacked in size. Even in its best days it was so poor that black bread and herring brine often made a full course dinner.

I suspect too that physically Seraye left something to be desired. Its houses were ramshackle, its streets unpaved. It was, all in all, a slum.

It had its limitations, Seraye did; but it had its virtues also, and quite extraordinary virtues.

There was piety in Seraye, intense, pure and exalted.

There was learning in Seraye, and reverance for learning. Bread might be scarce there, but not books. That village of near beggars supported a system of universal schooling and maintained a scholarship at Volozhin, the great Talmudical Academy of the district.

What is more, the townspeople of Seraye, as befitted disciples of the Scriptural prophets and rabbinic sages, had a keen sense of justice, so keen that, according to an ancient practice, anyone who had been wronged was entitled to interrupt public worship, holding it suspended until the inequity had been righted.

And it was a merciful place. The poorest of Seraye, even those who themselves lived on alms, gave something regularly for sweet charity's sake. Nor was its philanthropy merely formal. It sprang rather from spontaneous compassion, from that sense of *weltschmerz* which created the Hebrew phrase: *tsar baale hayyim,* "the pain of all living things."

And it was a place of a great spiritual earnestness.

Do not smile when I say this, but Seraye was very much like Boston and Concord in the days when New England was in flower.

The Kabbalist of Seraye, probing the mysteries of transcendentalism, what was he but a Hebraic Emerson? And the *Parush,* the scholarly recluse, was he not another Thoreau whose Walden chanced to be a corner of the *Yeshivah?*

That is why Jewish immigrants to this country came so quickly to understand Americanism. They needed only to translate the spirit of Seraye into English.

And now Seraye, at least the Jewish part of Seraye, is gone, wiped out, expunged by a ruthless hand almost to its last trace.

To be sure, I have no specific information about its fate. We do not yet know in detail what befell cities like Vilna or Suwalki. How then shall we have heard concerning villages?

And yet it is safe to venture a guess. After all, when evil men went about destroying a whole world, it is unlikely that they spared one tiny and insignificant corner of it, especially evil men so efficient in their wickedness.

Seraye is no more. Of that I am certain.

Its old, old, synagogue where my ancestors for uncounted generations worshiped God, is in ruins.

Of its Academy, where my father studied, nothing remains.

The books it composed and treasured, for which it dreamed, scrimped and saved, are now ashes.

Even its cemetery where my forefathers sleep has, I suppose, been erased.

And as for its Jews, of whom there were about two thousand in all—men, women and children, some saints, some sinners, some learned and some untutored, some wise and some foolish, but all eager to live, all undeserving of the fate which overtook them—I do not want to think of them. Especially I do not want to think of how most of them were done to death.

Yet think of them I must.

For, some of those Jews still live.

How many?

I do not know, of course. No one knows. Perhaps no one will ever know.

But there are probabilities and presumptions on which one can calculate.

We have learned for example that Jews in small towns fared much worse than those in the cities. They were so much more easily detected and apprehended; their opportunities for concealment were fewer. Besides, the non-Jews of Seraye, long schooled in anti-Semitism, would seem to have helped the Nazis in their job of extermination.

Let us, however, be optimists and say that, of two thousand Jews, as many as twenty came through alive.

These twenty Jews haunt me.

In the first place, I cannot figure out why they are they and I am I. Through what merit of mine am I safe, secure, free and light in heart whenever I watch my wife going about her household duties or hear my children laugh as they play? And what was their offense that they are cold, naked, hungry, haunted by horror? I simply cannot puzzle out what sin they committed so horrible as to merit the torments meted out to them; to look on while one's wife disappears into a death train or gas chamber, to see one's children spitted on bayonets, or to ponder their slow starvation, their bellies waxing great with bloatedness, their arms and legs turning matchstick thin, their bodies growing feeble with lassitude until life and death can no longer be told apart.

That is what haunts me: the thought that there, but for the grace of God and a capricious decision made by my father, but in any case through no virtue of mine, there go I, there my wife, there my children.

This thought, this morbid vagary if you prefer, takes on further poignancy when I reflect that, though I did not know them, some of those twenty Jews may very well be my remote kin. Who knows? Perhaps they bear the names common in our family—the Samuel to which my father answers, the Shraga Feivel, or Philip of one of my American cousins, the Jonathan of my son. What is more, being kin to me, they may actually resemble members of my family in both appearance and character. Perhaps one of them is short, limpid-eyed, and delicate as my Aunt Sarah was said to have been in her childhood, as her little American granddaughter, Alice, is today.

That is why these Jews haunt me; I feel that I know them and their lot.

After all, are they not flesh of my flesh, and blood of my blood?

✦

Twenty out of two thousand are still alive—if a word so suggestive of joy, vigor and hope can be applied to human wreckage.

Twenty out of two thousand, and these scattered to the four winds. A few are in Salzburg in the American zone of occupation, several in Bergen-Belsen in the British, one or two in Italy, a couple in France, one in Siberia, and one, of all places, in Shanghai.

And only yesterday a strange wonder occurred. Two Jews of Seraye wandering the streets of the internment camp at Theresienstadt unexpectedly came face to face with each other and cried out in one voice, "Merciful God, are *you* still alive?"

And then they wept heartbroken with the joy of a familiar face and the inconsolable grief of memory.

But the dispersion of the townspeople of Seraye is the least of their ruin.

Not one of them is sound in body. The starvation, torture and terror that wasted their frames, have ulcerated their stomachs, poisoned their kidneys, hardened the arteries of their brains and hearts, rotted the teeth out of their mouths, and so crippled and stunted their children that six-year-olds are often incapable of walking and ten-year-olds may be mere babies in structure. Nor is any of them "rosy cheeked"—unless it be with the flush of consumption.

Only one or two among them are actually insane. But every one of them is at least touched with madness—and some cannot sleep for the terrors that come in dreams by night.

Not one of them has a single garment beyond the rags on his back, the broken shoes and burlap wrappings on his feet.

Not one has a single possession—neither watch, nor fountain pen, nor scarf, nor coin.

Not one has a home, or shop, or a tool of his trade.

Not one has a newspaper to read, a prayerbook from which to worship God, a religious calendar to tell him which days are Sabbaths and Holy Days, a synagogue in which to pray.

Their children are unschooled, their young people untrained in crafts and skills.

Mention anything pertaining to life and its graces and they do not have it.

Of the twenty Jewish survivors of Seraye, three want to go back.

After all, one cannot stay in an internment camp forever.

And who knows, perhaps in Seraye by some miracle one will come upon a dearly loved and long despaired of wife or mother or child or friend.

Perhaps something remains of one's former home, or shop, or library or synagogue.

Then, too, there is the unfinished fight for freedom in Seraye—including freedom for Jews.

Besides, Seraye is home.

And so they are on the move—a tottering old woman from Switzerland, a young man from Lublin, a girl from a camp in Germany, half labor camp and half brothel.

These three need to be sustained now. Once they set out for home they will need more: provender on the way, protection from anti-Semites as they travel, Polish anti-Semites whom the Polish government has been unable to suppress, and Lithuanian anti-Semites whom not even the Soviet Army has brought to heel.

When they arrive at Seraye, the odds are the husband, wife, brother, friend will not be there. The home will be gone, the shop gone, the synagogue gone.

Then they will begin to require our help in earnest. They will need houses, shops, books, tools and since not so many as ten Jews are left to form a Minyan, they will need a synagogue at least in Suwalki, the county seat.

Of all the things they require both for the present and the future, they will have none unless we give it to them.

Which means the fullest support to the Joint Distribution Committee—the first participant in the United Jewish Appeal.

Of Seraye's Jews, seventeen will not go back to Seraye.

They will not go back for any one of many reasons; because they know that nothing remains in Seraye to which to return; because they can never again trust their neighbors who joined with the Nazis against them; because the streets of Seraye cry aloud of rape, murder and torture; because, despite all the efforts of the Red Army, there is more anti-Semitism in Seraye today than ever; because they are tired of defending themselves and apologizing for themselves; because they want to live normal lives.

Whatever the reason, they will not go back to Seraye.

Of these seventeen Jews, three have set their hearts on America. Though thanks to the quota system, only one will be so fortunate as ever to get here.

But for that one, American Jewry must be prepared, not only for his own sake but so that other lands may be encouraged also to open up their doors to homeless Jews. Which means the fullest support to the National Refugee Service—the second element in the United Jewish Appeal.

And as for the rest, fourteen out of twenty, they will go to one place, and one place only—to the land of their fathers, the place where refuge was promised to them by the nations of the world, to the Jewish Homeland, Eretz Yisrael.

Some are going to Palestine because there is literally no other place on earth for them; others because that is the only place where they are really wanted; still others, because, long before the Second World War, most of them had been made Zionists by the Jewish tradition, by the dream of a Judaism reborn and of historic Jewish ideals incarnated in the land which first gave them birth.

Observe, I do not say that they want to go to Palestine; I say they *are* going to Palestine.

They are going and nothing will stop them.

They will not be stopped by force of arms.

They will not be stopped by inane, pointless, time-consuming and, therefore, life-devouring investigations.

They will not be stopped, these Jews of Seraye.

And I am proud to say they are not being stopped.

One of them, a young vigorous man, is even now on a schooner Palestine bound. An old couple who wondrously have not only survived but remained unseparated, are trudging their way to a Yugoslav port, where, rumor has it, passage can be found. Two orphaned children in France scheme by day and night how they will make contact with the underground railway.

They may not all succeed, these Jews of Seraye.

But most of them will get through, and safely. They will get through because they must, because the alternative is slow death. They will get through because the right is on their side. And the right will not forever be denied. They will get through because they are going *home.*

They will get through. And when they do, we shall be able to rest more easily. Not only will they know at last what it means to be welcome and wanted, they will be participants in one of the most brilliant, creative and idealistic enterprises of modern times, the rebuilding of the Jewish National Home in Palestine, an enterprise which has revived, enriched, cleansed and modernized, for the benefit of *all* its inhabitants, a land long poverty stricken, sterile, retarded and disease-ridden; which has established an outpost of political and economic democracy in the feudal medievalism of the Near East; which has blazed trails toward more equitable and co-operative forms of group life; which has evoked an infinitely rich and colorful revival of Hebraic culture; which has converted Jews like the survivors of Seraye from pauperism to stalwart self-reliance, from a burden to themselves and a problem to the world into a social asset for all mankind.

All these wonderful things can and will come to pass—provided we do our fullest duty by the United Palestine Appeal, the third constituent agency of the United Jewish Appeal.

Let us think, then, on these twenty Jews of Seraye, and on the Jews of your own Serayes, human beings like yourselves, your own kith and kin. Let us reflect on the unspeakability of their present misery, on what they need to return to Seraye, or to come to America, or to go to Palestine. Can we delay for a moment our work of deliverance? Can we give to the United Jewish Appeal calculatingly, stintingly, on any scale less than our resources or their anguish?

We can, of course. It is physically possible for human beings to behave like beasts. But the one who so comports himself, if he has the least intimation of conscience, will not look comfortably into a mirror or ever think happily of the God who made him, singled him out for good fortune and bestowed on him so many benefits which he merits so little.

The Jews of Seraye, and of ten thousand places like Seraye, look to the United Jewish Appeal, that is to say, to us, for deliverance. That deliverance must be, and I am sure will be, speedy and full.

Such are my thoughts of Seraye.

With them and in their wake come all sorts and conditions of feelings.

Sometimes, when I think about Seraye, I am ashamed

to be a human being, ashamed to be member of a species which could perpetrate the evil done to Seraye, and almost as much ashamed of the supposedly good people of the world who stood by when the evil was being perpetrated, and who stand idle now.

Sometimes, when I think of Seraye, I want to hurl hard words at God, that terrible saying of Abraham: "Shall the Judge of the whole earth not do justice," that soul-searing inquiry of the prophet:

> "Thou, too pure of eyes to behold evil,
> Thou that canst not look on oppression,
> Wherefore hast thou looked on when
>   men did treachery
> And did hold Thy peace when the wicked
>   swallowed up the righteous?"

Sometimes, on the other hand, I want to slip into some synagogue and say Kaddish, the prayer for the dead, not the familiar Kaddish but the *Kaddish shel-Hasidim,* the Saints' Kaddish, as solemn as the other but with its grief more brightly illuminated by hope. I want to stand up and cry out over Seraye, over its dead, over its handful of living:

> *Yitgadal v'yitkaddash shmeh rabbah b'olmo di
> hu atid lehithadata.*

> "Magnified and sanctified be God's great name, in the world which He is to create anew, in which the dead will live, and life be eternal, and Jerusalem be rebuilt, and its shrine restored

193

and heathenism be uprooted and the worship of
the true God be set in its place, when the Holy
One blessed be He, will establish His Kingdom. . . ."

Baagalah uvizman kariv va-imru amen.

"Speedily and at a near time, and say ye, Amen."

Such are the mingled emotions that attend my thoughts
of Seraye. But through them all moves a two-fold resolution that is always with me, that never falters nor fails,
no matter what else I may be thinking or feeling.

I am resolved that, so far as lies within my power, those
Jews of Seraye shall, at long last, have justice done them.

Which means, that those who want to go back to Seraye
shall have the right to do so without hindrance, and shall
enjoy security, freedom and equality, when they have
come home at last; which means further that those on the
other hand who want to go to Palestine shall have *that*
right without hindrance and shall enjoy security, freedom
and equality when *they* have come home at last.

This is one resolution.

And the other is that, so far as lies within my power,
those Jews shall have everything they require to survive
and to rebuild their lives; that at no moment, if I can prevent it, will they lack for food, clothing, shelter, medical
and psychiatric care or the things that minister to the
spirit.

Shall I attempt to catch in two words, almost two gestures, all the complex, subtle, terrible and exalted things

194

I think and feel when I think of Seraye and its Jews, living and dead—thoughts and feelings which I know you share since you would not otherwise be worthy to be fashioned in human form or to be called Jews?

We feel together, you and I, the will to *fight* and the will to *give,* to fight until justice is accomplished, to give until mercy is done.

These then are our final and deepest thoughts in all our thinking about Seraye, your Seraye and mine.

FIGHT—and GIVE!

CHAPTER 12

LATTER DAY MIRACLES: ISRAEL *

SHALL a miracle be performed in the sight of men and they fail to marvel or neglect to speak of it?

During the past year a miracle has been performed before our eyes. The State of Israel has come into being, come into being in defiance of all reasonable expectation. It is of this that I wish to speak today. First because being a miracle it requires to be spoken of. And second because no other theme is possible in a Jewish pulpit on the first Rosh Hashanah after so epochal and breathtaking an event.

To be sure our joyous wonder over it is already somewhat abated. It has so soon been dimmed by custom, chilled by unanticipated problems which have opened up.

But dimmed and chilled though it be, it remains a wondrous event, more wondrous by far than is generally perceived.

For the coming home of Israel after eighty long generations seems to me more than what it is usually taken for. It is more than a victory of justice over brute force, though it is that; more than an advance of democracy

* Rosh Hashanah Sermon, October, 1948.

over feudalism; more than a promise to D.P.'s that their time of servitude is at its end; more than the beginning of the final solution of the age-old problem of Jewish homelessness; more than a new lease on life for Judaism both in Palestine and elsewhere.

All these are precious and radiant things. Yet there is something more and greater in the birth of Israel than any of them or all of them together, something of concern not only to Jew but to all men, something not political or economic or cultural in character but spiritual, nothing less than the demonstration of a universal, vital, joyous truth concerning human existence, the truth of the ever-present possibility in life of the miraculous.

For I was not speaking loosely when I used the word miracle in connection with the establishment of the Jewish State. I meant that word literally, though in a very particular sense.

The word miracle has four possible significances.

Most commonly it denotes the supernatural, that which is supposed to happen contrary to nature and its laws. It suggests to Jews events such as Joshua's stopping of the sun; to Christians, Jesus walking on the waters of the Sea of Galilee; to Catholics among Christians, a Saint Sebastian picking up his decapitated head and walking away with it.

Once everyone believed that events on this order could occur, when men disputed only over the conflicting claims entered by the various faiths, each on behalf of its own miracles.

For almost all of us as modern men such a belief is an

impossibility. We look on all tales of breaches of nature, including those of Scripture, as folklore. In this sense then the word miracle has no relevance for us either to Palestine or anything else.

There is a second meaning to the concept, the esthetic. For example, I contemplate the blush of a rose or the flight of a bird or the smile of a baby and cry out: this is miraculous. By which I mean that it is moving beyond all expectation, so mysterious that I cannot fathom it, too wonderful or beautiful perhaps to be endured at all. In this sense the birth of Israel may be regarded as a miracle. But this is a limited and not too consequential application of the word; it is included in the meaning I have in mind, but only as a small part of it.

Another significance of the word is to be seen in the following illustration. Among the diseases that affect man there are some which have always been fatal. Now let us imagine a person suffering from such an ailment who has just resigned himself to death when announcement is made of a new and certain therapy. Will this not appear to him and to those who love him as a miracle? And yet to term it that is to use the word loosely indeed. For what has happened is obviously no more than a happy coincidence.

But here let us tread softly. For we stand now at the verge of something else, something radically different.

Suppose our hypothetical patient is one of those persons—medical annals are full of his like—who refuse to die on schedule. It has been said of him by his physicians that he cannot possibly live beyond a certain time, but his is an inordinate love of life, or he has some job to see through, and by sheer will power he has kept going not only longer than has been expected but long enough for the new remedy to save his life. Here we have no breach of natural law, but here obviously we have more than pure coincidence. What we are dealing with now is a conquest by the will of circumstances which objectively regarded are insuperable; it is the achievement by spirit of what by every law of logic and common sense seems impossible. But when the immovable is moved, when the insuperable is conquered, and the impossible is achieved, what else is that but a miracle?

And that is exactly what is involved in the State of Israel. It represents an achievement by spirit of the impossible.

The impossible, not merely the unlikely or implausible or improbable, but, and again I am being careful with my words, that which by every rule of reason was impossible.

There is much in the birth of Israel which is wonderful without being impossible.

The political victory before the United Nations, against initial odds that were overwhelming. The courage of those who penetrated Nazi Europe for the rescue of their brethren, of those who manned the underground railway and seaway for the smuggling in of immigrants and arms, of those on the *Exodus 1947*, who sweated out their unequal struggle with the British Empire. The dazzling bravery, ingenuity, selflessness—and the incredible outcome—of Jewish self-defense against Arab onslaught and the world's indifference. All these are wonderful enough. They constitute a saga of intrepidity to be set alongside of, yes, even above, the Maccabees and Thermopylae, Valley Forge and the Battle of Britain. Wonderful, breathtakingly wonderful, but not impossible.

So also with what the Jews of Palestine have made of the waste soil of their land, of the Rip Van Winkle Hebrew language, of Jewish culture, of their social life and, most marvelous of all, themselves.

Again, these, seen in advance, might have appeared improbable, even fantastically so, but not impossible. And yet in the arising of Israel there were achieved in actual, cold, sober fact not one but three impossibilities.

The first of these is the survival of Israel itself.

This is an old wonder, centuries old; therefore we take it for granted. It is a quiet, unspectacular wonder, therefore we pay it no heed. But if a man would perceive how wonderful it is, how actually impossible, then let him transport himself in imagination back 1,878 years, to the year 70, and stand where Israel stood then, after its dreadful defeat in the war with Rome; one fifth of its numbers dead, another fifth sold into slavery, the land lost, the Temple lost, the Sanhedrin lost, the schools lost, everything lost. What odds would he have given for the survival of this people? Had there ever been till then, would there ever be in all history, a single instance of a people living on without its land, let alone after such vast losses?

Then suppose he had foreseen that not in nineteen centuries—twice as long as the entire career of the Roman Empire—would a return be possible, that meantime this people would be subjected to massacre, expulsion, expropriation, to every conceivable cruelty, humiliation, and disability at the hands of every nation, church, and class among whom it sought refuge.

Suppose a man had known all this 1,878 years ago: what verdict would be pronounced concerning the possibility of survival of this people? What would he have said? Then let us hear what is being said, now, after the event.

The great Russian theologian, Nicholas Berdyaev pronounced bluntly: "The continued existence of Jewry down the centuries is rationally inexplicable."

Berdyaev, it may be objected, is a theologian interested in establishing Israel as a mystery among the mysteries of Christian doctrine, perhaps being a theologian disposed to make mysteries of very plain things. Then let us hear what a sociologist has to say: "By every sociological law," writes Carl Mayer, "the Jews should have perished long ago."

This then is one miracle of Israel, one achievement by it of that which is logically impossible, its survival in the flesh. Its survival in the spirit is no less miraculous.

It happens sometimes that an individual or a people undergoes intolerable hardships yet does not perish, continuing to live, but on a subhuman level, like some of the prisoners in Nazi concentration camps who were reduced to groveling beasts; like, among peoples, the gypsies or the untouchables of India.

To such a state, by every rule of reason, the Jews should have been reduced, to a wolf pack, a people of outlaws, soulless Golems. Yet that is just what they did not become. On the contrary they remained not only human but cultivated and humane, both as individuals and a group, and that is the second of our miracles.

And that they remembered the land is the third.

How long can a people be expected to remember anything, to cherish a constitution, to honor a treaty, to keep a vow, especially when it has ceased to profit them? A generation? A century? Unlikely. A millennium? Impossible. Well, this people by the waters of Babylon swore: If I forget thee, O Jerusalem.

That was twenty-six centuries, more than two and a half millennia ago, yet it did not forget.

Not in all history has any people remembered anything so long a time as this. Nor is the mere perseverance of the memory, the whole of the wonder. That Jews should have thought of Zion in times of distress when the places where they dwelt were bleak and inhospitable—that is understandable. But how shall one account for a Yehudah Halevi singing in the bright tranquility of medieval Spain:

> My heart is in the East,
>   and I in the furthermost West
> How shall I find savor in what I eat,
>   how shall it be pleasant?

How account for him, and for Enzo Sereni in pre-Fascist Italy, for Hannah Senesh in pre-Nazi Hungary, for Emma Lazarus and Jesse Sampter and Louis Brandeis and Henrietta Szold in America, for all those who lived amidst quietude and comfort and security and still did not forget?

This then is the miracle I see in the birth of Israel, or more exactly in what lies beyond and behind it, the three-fold miracle of the survival of the people, of its soul, of its remembering. This is no miracle in the traditional sense. No seas divided to bring it to pass, no flame descended from heaven, no angels appeared. All that happened was that by the spirit a people achieved the impossible. Merely that and nothing more.

Now miracles, even if unattended by signs from on high, are not so common as to go unnoticed. If only out of curiosity we ought to look closely at the one with which we have been privileged.

But there is a second, more urgent reason for such an examination. Heaven knows, mankind right now could use a few timely and apposite miracles. With East and West circling warily about each other; with the atom bomb hanging heavy over our heads; with social justice and political liberty more precariously balanced than ever before; with class and racial hatred more bitter and ex-plosive than ever; with our hearts sinking ever deeper into skepticism, passivity, despair—in this intolerable dilemma, this impossible situation, we could employ a few miracles to very considerable advantage.

Only—only how does one go about creating miracles? Well, let us inspect the one which is currently before us and see what we can learn from it.

How was the great Jewish miracle of our day brought to pass?

First, by *hope*. To this our forefathers clung, even when it seemed altogether hopeless. By education and preaching they imparted hope to one another; by their observances they bolstered it and made it dynamic. Deliberately, calculatingly, they made themselves prisoners of hope, too enthralled by it ever to be disenchanted.

Of their hope, furthermore, be it observed that it was a hope born of love, love of people and land, of man and God. Had it been the creature of hate, as was that of Hitler, it could not have lasted so long, for hate destroys not only its objects but those who tolerate it. It eats them up alive until they and their hope are both consumed into nothingness. Only love endures, only love gives life. When then one speaks of the staying power of hope, let it be understood that that hope is for life, not death; for good, not evil.

What is more, they never allowed hope to remain only hope, a mere yearning and wishing. At every opportunity they converted it into *will* and *effort*.

It is a common misconception that all through the centuries the Jews sat still and waited for the Messiah to realize their hope for them. Nothing could be more mistaken. Actually, there was never a time when Palestine was without Avelay Zion, as pre-Zionist settlers called themselves. To be sure, they did not use modern techniques of political negotiation and planned settlement. But they never stopped trying. At the first favorable turn in Palestine, immigration was instantly afoot. Only, their strength was slight and circumstance was always against them, so that they never achieved anything very much, and often it seemed that they never would.

But here let me say something about the struggle

between circumstance and will. Circumstance is the combined weight of all the things and forces which make up the exterior world, and will is just the feeble energy of man's resolved heart. But circumstance is always shifting; change is its law. Therefore it does not matter how powerful circumstance may be or how adverse, the will, if only it persists, will get its opportunity against it.

Consider seeds falling on a sheet of bedrock and struggling to root themselves. The stone does not yield. It is impossible that any living thing establish itself here. But the rains fall constantly, the winds blow, the sun shines, heating the rock, then night comes and it cools. Sometimes, even if only for a fleeting instant, a fissure will appear in this unyielding rock. Then the seeds will have their way at last, provided that they are present at the appropriate moment. To this end the seeds must keep falling all the long, apparently hopeless seasons and years so that, though they be wasted by millions, there may be a seed waiting when the rock cracks.

So it was with our people and Palestine. Two thousand years of constant trying, and always circumstances were prohibitive. Then for a short while, a few decades, conditions turned, if not favorable then indifferent. For a moment in an eternity there was a chance. But for that moment Israel was waiting, waiting and ready. That is how miracles are made, how the impossible is achieved. A constant, never-ending pressure against the wall of circumstance; until in its shifting an opening appears and a break-through is achieved.

But what are the implications here not only for Jews

but for all mankind? Shall we not see that if one miracle can be wrought, then others are workable also. If the spirit can achieve one supposed impossibility then of nothing can it be said that it is impossible. On Kol Nidre night, and in another frame of reference, I shall apply this thesis, demonstrated by Israel, to the problems of our individual inner lives. But let me confine myself right now to the social scene. If our miracle could be brought to pass then there is no communal good of which we need despair.

The liberation of the Negro from his tragic plight in American life, the emancipation of the world's colonial peoples from the degradation and exploitation which have been their lot, the winning of political freedom in totalitarian states, the achievement of economic justice everywhere—is any of these any more difficult than that Israel should have survived and come home?

Yes, even the achievement of world government, of an enduring peace, enforced by law, among nations, that good which of all boons now seems to us, in our alarm and disillusionment over the East-West crisis, the most hopeless of all—is even that impasse any harder to overcome than that through which Israel broke?

To be sure, these are hard, bitter, stubborn evils, those which I have enumerated. Deep instincts in man and powerful forces in society give them strength. Yet mankind's chances of conquering them are better, even in this dark hour of international explosiveness, than Israel's were for regaining its land at any time in nineteen hundred years.

Israel in its cause has always had to stand alone against

the entire world, with not an ally by its side. These other causes have the support of millions belonging to all races and classes.

Israel's dream never for a moment in all those nineteen hundred years came anywhere near close to fulfillment; on these other issues substantial progress has already been made.

Again, let us consider how recent is the struggle for these social ideals, not as visions and ideals—in this sense they are as old as the prophets—but as practical tasks to which men in numbers apply themselves seriously. The effort for the emancipation of the Negro is a century old; for the liberation of colonial peoples less than that; for political democracy three centuries; for economic justice as a comprehensive design embracing all men newer even than that; and world government no more ancient than a few generations. Israel had to wait nineteen centuries. Shall we in these other causes lose patience so soon?

And especially now, when science is putting into our hands the most promising tool perhaps in all man's career, the new dynamic psychology which by uncovering the causes of mental sickness both in individuals and nations gives hope for its control, for the early spotting and curing of such a demonism as possessed Hitler, such psychic malformations as crippled and perverted the German people.

If only mankind has enough time—

But will it? What if the atom bomb is dropped first?

If that should happen, alas for the life, joy, and re- sources that will be wasted, alas for the generations, perhaps centuries of postponement of the good society. But even then, it need not be the end. Man is incredibly tough and resilient. He wills to live and the will, as we have just seen, has a way of getting its way.

Only, it should not, it must not come to that, to all that damage and delay. The bomb must not fall. Everything, literally everything except surrender to intimidation and injustice, must be tried first. If only we are patient enough and press hard enough, we may find a peaceable way out. The iron curtain dividing East and West is high and fearsomely strong, but it is no higher or harder than that which stood between Israel and its land. If one could be penetrated then the other can be breached also. The outcome depends not on the barriers but on the spirit that beats against them, how long, how mightily, and how unrelentingly it beats.

This then is the deeper, universal significance of the birth of the State of Israel. It proves that if only a hope be good, born of love and justice, if only it remain not hope but become will and effort, if only it press unceasingly against adverse circumstance, the hope must be fulfilled in the end. It demonstrates in a word that the age of miracles is not over, that to spirit all things are possible.

Perhaps it is because I am a theologian by profession that I see in our event still one more meaning—so far enumerated, something of philosophical import, something that throws a clear, unexpected light on the deepest riddle haunting man; the riddle of the nature of reality.

We have just had an extraordinary experience. With our own eyes, we have seen spirit, the spirit of a small, powerless people, achieve a mighty thing, an impossible thing.

Now I ask: What kind of a universe would it seem to be in which spirit, so long as it seeks the good, can in the end prove so powerful? Does this not appear a universe responsive to spirit and therefore spirit animated?

This then is the final, deepest, most universal significance of all in this surpassing wonder, this beautiful, blessed event of the home coming of our people after eighty generations.

It argues for God; it affirms by implication the supreme thesis—that over nature, over man and over human affairs, Spirit reigns supreme, that God is King.

One of the most haunting of all rabbinic conceptions is that of *Ikvoth ha-Mashiach*, the footsteps of the Messiah, the foreshadowing tokens of the coming of God's Kingdom on earth.

Among these premonitory signs by ancient tradition Israel's return to Zion is one of the most significant.

But why should the deliverance of one small people and its land be an augury of the redemption of all mankind?

Because, to our fathers, though they believed implicitly in these two events, both seemed equally impossible, equally to require the intervention of miracles.

Wherefore, they argued, when one came to be, when the smaller miracle had been performed, was not this the time to be hopeful of the other, larger also?

This then is my warrant for saying, even in the gloom of this hour, be strong and of good heart; gird up your loins, make resolute your arms, put your shoulders with all the might at your command against the walls that keep the Messiah out. And all this with high, fair hope.

For once, a short while ago, there were two impossibilities: that Israel return and that the Kingdom come.

Now only one remains, the other having been achieved.

Do your ears not detect in that fact the *Ikvoth ha-Mashiach*, the sound, faint yet clear, distant but nearing, of the oncoming steps of the Messiah, the King?

IV

JUDAISM
AND THE PERSONAL LIFE

CHAPTER 13

OUR PERSISTENT FAILURES

☀☀☀☀☀☀☀☀☀☀☀☀☀☀☀☀☀☀☀☀☀☀☀☀☀☀☀☀☀

O F THE Hasidic Saint, Levi Yitzhak of Berditchev, it is related that once, during the solemn period between New Year and the Day of Atonement, he stood at the door of his house, dull, lifeless, altogether out of tune with the season, lethargic under all calls to penitence.

And as he stood so, a cobbler came by, looking for work. Spying the rabbi he called:

Have you nothing that needs mending?

Have I nothing that needs mending? Levi Yitzhak echoed reflectively. Then his heart contracted within him and he wept.

He wept for his sins, for all those things in his soul and life that needed mending, the scuffed places, the split seams, the rundown edges, the holes, of which, being a saint and hence an expert on the state of souls, he was well aware.

Only, why, instead of weeping, did he not do with his soul as he would with his shoes? Why did he not get busy at once making the necessary repairs?

Do you not suppose he had tried to do just that, not

once but many times? How often had he not said to himself concerning something defective in himself or his circumstances: this cannot go on, I will not allow it. But though he meant what he said, though he swore to it, whatever it was which needed mending too often proved stronger than his will or ability to mend it. Therefore he wept, not so much for his failings, as for the failure of his efforts to right them.

Well might he weep over this tragedy of his moral life, the repeated defeat of his will to better things, and well would we do to weep with him—we whose souls are shabbier than his, whose resolutions to repair them are less frequent, less earnest, less passionate, whose failures are more nearly total.

What the sins and deficiencies of that saint may have been which he was always trying to right but never quite succeeding I cannot imagine. Perhaps when he had been young he had known illicit desires. Perhaps later his mind wandered at times when he prayed. Perhaps once when he preached he had been more interested in the plaudits of men than in the cause of God. Perhaps at times he found himself proud of his repute or self-complacent over his virtues.

But as for us, we exhibit among us virtually every sin and deficiency in the book except perhaps for a few of the most flagrant and violent. There is scarcely a line in the confession, aside from those dealing with crimes like murder, which does not strike home with somebody. What is more, every one of us has his own special vices and inadequacies.

How then shall I deal with this theme relevantly to all of us at one time, seeing that though we are all offenders our offenses are different? Let me select one or two or three fairly common human weaknesses and order my argument about these; if I strike one man's special deformities he need only attend to what I say; and if I miss another's peculiar weakness, let him make the necessary adaptations to his own situation.

This then is the question before us: What shall we do about the persistent failure of all our attempts at self-improvement?

What of those among us who are creatures of envy, who cannot look on the good fortune of another without being stabbed to the quick with jealousy, and uttering some malicious and derogatory remark; who, every time they so respond, despise themselves and resolve next time to keep their feelings under control, or if not their feelings then at least their tongues?

And what of those whose failing is a triggerlike temper, a flaring of irritability at the least provocation, who are at such moments burdens to their husbands or wives, monsters to their children, terrors to their employees, who have sworn seven times seventy to restrain themselves under the next provocation, and they have not done so?

And what of those who want to be generous but cannot, who skimp on their contributions to charity, always giving less than they can afford, as little as they can get away with, and yet not happy when they have their way, knowing as they do that a man, if he is to respect himself, must at least on occasion throw calculation to the

215

winds and act recklessly? Wherefore they are forever promising themselves, and with utmost earnestness, that it will be different. Still the same sorry story of scheming, dodging, crawling.

All these are assembled here on this Day of Atonement—the envy-ridden, the trigger-tempered, the ungenerous, and with them the hateful, the proud, the lusting, and the lying, the attention-demanding and the cowardly, the arrogant and the cringing—and who not else?—each aware not only of the peculiar blemishes of his soul but even more painfully of the failure of his so many attempts to rectify them. And our mood, now that I have reminded each of you of his own private deformities and defeats—what else can it be but grim? And then, into our unhappiness comes the Yom Kippur message—for all the world like some gay chatterbox into a house of mourning. For though this day be solemn, its point is as blithe as can be conceived; it asserts brightly that there is not a scuffed place in our lives we cannot mend. But we know or think we know otherwise. And so, if we are cynical we smile wearily to hear this day's message; if resigned, we simply disregard it; if still aching with our disappointments we wince, salt is being poured on our wounds. But whether it be one or the other, we sit here, some for the purpose of seeing and being seen, some out of filial piety, others out of Jewish loyalty, but all too few out of a living faith in what this day represents.

How can we ignore the urgency in the problem of our persistent failures? The seriousness, the meaningfulness, the vindication of the Yom Kippur observance in which

216

we are now engaged depend on whether we can resolve this problem. But, greater and more important, the hopefulness of our entire lives is involved. For how shall men live joyously if they are forever to be the prisoners of what they have always been, if the crooked in them can never be made straight, if our past is forever to be a morgue for the corpses of good intentions, a charnel house in which our hopes for better things rot noisomely?

Well, what shall we do with our persistent and repeated failures?

Since it was Levi Yitzhak who raised the issue to begin with, let us consider how he himself dealt with it.

It is said that in his latter years he adopted the following practice. Each night on retiring he would review his day and say of whatever was evil in it—

"I shall not do so again."

Having said this, he would continue his soliloquy.

"But so you promised last night and the night before."

"Ah yes," he would answer himself, "but tonight I am in earnest."

A naïve, perhaps even a pointless anecdote, and not, it would seem at first glance, very hopeful, nor at all consistent with the man's reputation for wisdom. Well, if Levi Yitzhak cannot help us, we shall have to get along without him. Let us see what devices we can invent for ourselves, what counsels aside from Levi Yitzhak's are available to us.

There is first of all the advice offered by the realists among us, by the realist in each of us. It consists in the plain proposition that if we cannot adjust our conduct to our ideals then we might do well to adjust our ideals to our conduct.

Perhaps, says the realist, the trouble with our lives is that we are excessively idealistic. Having first set our goals too high for our reach, shall we then be dismayed when inevitably we fall short of them? A little more practicality, if you please. Put your goals a little lower, where they will be within your reach, and then you will reach them.

Which sounds at first like pure reasonableness, but only until one examines the proposal a little more closely.

For, in the first place, if we are typically human we have already lowered our sights without waiting for any-one to suggest it to us. Our difficulty is not that we insist on some ideal maximum but that having compromised on a minimum we fail even of that.

Our man of envy, for example, is not bothered by the fact that he is not constantly full of love and benevolence for everyone—which he no longer expects of himself—but that he is always alive with jealousy.

The dilemma of our skimping contributor is not that he does not give away all that he has but that he cannot bring himself to give away even as much as he can well afford.

The proposal of the realist, in other words, turns out in the end to be irrelevant, inapplicable, unworkable, in brief, unrealistic.

And it is dangerous too. For in effect it means that every time we fail we shall lower our standards. But having done that once we are likely to do it again and again with each failure, until in the end we are left with none at all.

No, there is no exit from our dilemma by this device of compromising our ideals. The realist unable to help us falls silent; whereupon another voice sounds in our ears, that of the cynic in our midst, within our own hearts.

Give it up, it bids us, this whole striving after wind, for that is what ideals are, not only unattainables, but delusions and, even worse, sources of discontent and bitterness within us, forever awakening hungers that cannot be satisfied. Give it up and have peace at last.

But if we do so, we ask the cynic, by what and for what shall we live? A ship can drift rudderless, sailless, compassless, until it founders. But we are no inanimate things to be swept now here now there by the chance winds of mood and circumstance. We have feelings, hopes, fears, preferences. Besides, decisions are required of us. If we give up all ideals, on what basis shall we make decisions?

Well then, the cynic concedes, perhaps you will need some guiding principles, some goals; you will almost certainly want to be free from pain and insecurity; you will want to enjoy life's pleasures. Allow yourself then such minimal purposes, but only such.

But in that case, how are we better off than before? Again we have ideals, except that now we call them guiding principles and goals. The only difference wrought by the cynic's cynicism is that if we follow his advice, our goals will be shabbier than otherwise, we shall have set our hearts on tawdry, selfish purposes and shall be as much in danger of missing these as better purposes. Assuredly, if one must gamble against defeat in any case, he may as well play for higher, more honorable stakes.

Besides, can we really follow the cynic's counsel? Can we, no matter how we try, actually give up the most cherished of human values, truth, goodness, beauty, love? Will they not continue to haunt us? *Es redt sich so,* this business of renouncing ideals. Actually, against all will and reason they continue to haunt men, even the most cynical of men. What then is the sense of a policy which proceeds from an impossible first premise, which calls on men to do that of which, try as they will, they are not capable?

But now we are in a bad way indeed. We have worked ourselves into a position in which there are only three possible courses of action and none of these is tenable. We cannot achieve our ideals; we cannot compromise them; we cannot surrender them. Then what else remains?

Though it probably would not occur to us, there is still another proposed solution of our problem to be considered, that advanced by Paul, Augustine, Calvin, Luther, by the main Christian tradition. For it is just from a judgment of despair over man's moral plight that essential Christianity springs. Man, Christianity teaches, is under the obligation to do God's will which, since it is God's will, he may neither repudiate or tamper with. But man, being man, is necessarily sinful and cannot do God's will as is required of him. Therefore he would be altogether lost and damned, were it not that God took on flesh in the shape of Jesus Christ who, being God and free from sin, can fulfill the law, and who, by becoming human and dying on behalf of men, redeems them from the damnation to which they are otherwise predestined.

Need I, a rabbi, say here in a synagogue on Kol Nidre night, that whatever its value to Christians this doctrine is no solution for us who are Jews?

I pass over the fact that is totally unacceptable to the Jewish spirit not only because it assumes that a man once existed who was also God, but also because it affirms the dogma of vicarious atonement, the thesis that one man's sinfulness can be purged by the actions of someone else, a position against which Judaism has always held that though men can help one another morally, each man must in the end save his own soul. I pass over this and other similar considerations. This is neither the time nor place to engage in theological controversy. Besides the issue before us is one of practice not theory. But it is just here in practice that the classic Christian doctrine breaks down. For suppose, for argument's sake, that our jealousy-ridden brother accepts it. I am a sinful creature, he confesses on his knees, unable to redeem myself from my vice of envy. But God so loved me that he sent his only begotten son to die on the cross that his blood might redeem me.

Having spoken so, he rises again to his feet. And lo, his original problem is with him as pressingly as before. What is he to do with himself and the envy that surges up in him when good fortune again befalls someone round about him?

Now we are in an even worse dilemma than before. Having considered and rejected the proposal that we moderate our ideals; having considered and rejected the proposal that we surrender them altogether, we finally considered the proposal that we depend on someone else to achieve them for us, only to be compelled to reject that also. But this ends the list of possible proposals—that is—except for the proposal of Levi Yitzhak, which seemed so trivial that we simply brushed it aside. Perhaps now we would be well advised to return to it. After all the man does enjoy a great reputation for wisdom. Besides, since we are at the end of our own resources, what do we stand to lose?

What is it then which Levi Yitzhak used to do when he considered his failings? He resolved not to fail again! And what, when he remembered other pledges made to this effect and broken? He did not play the realist and seek to reduce his commitments, nor the cynic and surrender them, nor the Christian and look about for someone else to fulfill them for him. Instead he stood by his ideals full and uncompromised and pledged to attain them, resolutely, hopefully, as though it were for the first time, as though he had never resolved it before only to be defeated.

So once, so again, so a hundred times, a thousand, a myriad, an infinity of times.

But to what end or purpose? Can any good come out of multiplying failures?

Yes, Levi Yitzhak would say, many things.

In the first place it is better to fail in some good cause than to succeed in an evil one. For so at least the honor of man is salvaged, his moral integrity is preserved.

On this point Levi Yitzhak, the medieval Jew, would have agreed wholeheartedly with the modern Jew, Louis Untermeyer, when he prayed:

God, give me the heart to fight—and lose.

Besides, Levi Yitzhak would continue, even if we achieve nothing positive by our constant struggle, think what we avert.

Our niggardly contributor may never get around to that generosity he has so often promised; but had he quit making promises he would by now be skimping more shamefully than ever.

Our trigger-tempered brother still breaks out in temper tantrums, but can you imagine how much more frequent and savage they would be had he come to accept them without protest?

At the least and worst then, our striving on in the teeth of all our failures, if it does not make us better, may keep us from becoming worse.

But there is something more that may be won.

Speaking recently of the miracle of Israel reborn, I said that spirit, if only it continue to press long enough against the wall of confining circumstance, must in the end break through to fulfillment. So it was with the people of Israel which after seventy-nine generations of failure won its victory on the eightieth. Are we to suppose it is much different with man's inner life?

Here in the depths of man's heart burns a moral will, and hedging it in are all the barriers thrown up by indolence and evil habit. For the individual spirit these walls inside him may be as formidable as the walls of outer circumstance for a group, and he has a shorter time to work out his destiny. But the walls within like the walls without are creatures of time and subject to change. If then only the pressure of spirit continues, any next moment may bring what has so long been denied—a breakthrough.

The man of quick anger may for once, perhaps under the wildest provocation, prove gentle, patient, forbearing.

And he who has never before succeeded in being truly generous may achieve a self-forgetfulness, a reckless abandon on behalf of some cause beyond himself.

For one who effects such a break-through of the spirit the rabbis had a special name. They called him "he who acquires eternity in one flash." They tell of one such, an executioner who in all his life had never disclosed the faintest trace of compassion but in whom pity surged once so suddenly and assertively that he gave up his life to ease the suffering of Rabbi Hananyah ben Teradyon who lay before him on the rack.

Another such was Nathan d'Zuzitha, a sensualist who had never denied himself anything, until the day when in an explosion of latent decency he renounced the woman whom he desired so fiercely that there was no alternative to her but his death.

These are admittedly melodramatic episodes which the rabbis have recorded and handed down, but who does not know from his own experience of less spectacular instances of the pent-up spirit erupting, of cowards carrying off acts of unexpected heroism; of the hateful overflowing, even if briefly, with love, of the calloused displaying compassion.

A break-through then is always possible, and once it has occurred two things are forever after different. In the first place, both in his own eyes and in the eyes of others, he who has engineered the break-through takes on a new guise. He has ceased to be the always irritable or cruel or calculating—he is now the sometimes patient, or merciful, or selfless.

What is more, if one break-through can be made, then a second or third, a tenth or hundredth is possible. Indeed, with each penetration, the breach becomes wider and wider until it is a broad avenue through which the spirit marches effortlessly. But when that has happened, and on a sufficiently important trait, do you know what has become of our struggler? He has turned into a saint.

For the saint is not different in natural endowment from you or me. He too is by nature irritable and lustful and prideful and selfish and calculating. What sets him apart from the rest of men is that he has pierced the wall of base instinct and evil practice so often and so mightily that getting through has become a habit with him.

But even if not, even if the outcome is nothing—no saintliness, no break-throughs, perhaps not even such a negative gain as preventing some other evil—even then Levi Yitzhak would insist on his program of unrelenting effort.

For to him the good for which he strove and from which he fell short was not a matter of his preference. It was, to be sure, an objective which he had selected and set up for himself, but it was also and more fundamentally a commandment of his God; an order from his master on high, which, being a faithful servant, he had no choice but to obey.

But this is the bedrock not alone of Levi Yitzhak's position but of our own as well as all other religious people. Even of those of us who insist that they are irreligious.

Why, in fact, do we keep reasserting our ideals despite all our failures? In part because our sense of dignity as human beings allows nothing else, in part because we recognize that so we obviate other evils, in part because we hope for a break-through, even that succession of break-throughs which is saintliness, but most of all because the ideal will not let us go. Justice, mercy, truth, tolerance, generosity, selflessness are for us as for Levi Yitzhak not matters of choice but inescapable, uncompromisable mandates which we can no more escape than Jonah could when he fled to Tarshish or Francis Thompson when he sought to elude the Hound of Heaven. If we are religiously minded, we talk about divine commandments; if secularly, about ethical imperatives. In all cases we are pointing to the same thing: the greatest wonder exhibited by man: that as a magnetic needle is drawn northward so he is drawn, inexorably, to the good, the true, and the beautiful. The secularists among you may account for this as you please. To me as a religionist the explanation seems very clear. This drive of man toward the good, what is it but the propulsion of God pushing relentlessly against us as we push against circumstance, so that all our separate pushings become in the end individualized fragments of the infinite push of the Divine.

What then shall we do about our failures?

What but keep on trying?

And if you ask why, I can give you many reasons. But in the end there is only one. We have no choice in the matter. God allows us none.

We have followed Levi Yitzhak, and he has proved a dependable guide. Is it possible that he can give us not only guidance for our thought and action but solace for our defeats as well, that he can say something which shall ease the pain and shame of our failures?

Yes, that too.

To be sure, we need not turn to him. Other, earlier rabbis have also spoken words of comfort on that score.

Is it not written:

"Not thine to finish the work, but neither art thou free to desist from it?"

Is it not written further:

"Alike are he who achieves much and he who achieves little, if but the hearts of the two be equally directed to the service of heaven?"

And Levi Yitzhak who has said so many things surpassingly well has spoken exquisitely on this also.

Speaking of the palm branches of Succoth, the festival next after the Day of Atonement, and interpreting them, like the ancient rabbis, as palms of victory; noting also that *all* Jews were commanded to take them in hand, and not the saintly Jews only, or the learned, Levi Yitzhak commented as follows:

It is as when a king sends forth his army to battle and to one commander gives great forces against a weak enemy so that he prevails easily, but to another slight forces against a mighty foe, so that he wins no engagements and is fortunate not to be overthrown in battle altogether. Now when the two commanders return home one is cheered by the multitude and the other ignored. Not so the king. He distributes the palms to all his army equally, but in his heart he cherishes one or the other not as does the multitude according to victories and defeats, but by what to him is of greater account than these, the sturdiness and devotion with which each man has fought on his behalf.

Therefore is it commanded on Succoth, the festival after Yom Kippur, that each man, and not only the learned and pious, shall take in hand the palm branch of the Lulav. For when he does so, each man knows in his own heart— and knows also that God knows—whether he has so fought as to deserve to carry the emblem of victory of his God.

CHAPTER 14

A PITY FOR THE LIVING

THERE are some verses which the ancient rabbis used to describe thus: "The verse comes and says: Preach about me!" It is just such a passage that I have in mind now, and a most unconventional text it is, being neither Biblical verse nor Talmudical epigram, but a modern short story—that poignant Yiddish tale by Sholom Aleichem entitled *A Pity for the Living*.

Here, abbreviated and condensed, is Sholom Aleichem's story:

On the eve of a holiday a distracted mother says to her little boy,

"Here, here is some horse-radish for you to grate. But close your eyes, you little fool, because if I find you crying I'll smack you."

"Why does she have to call me a fool?" the child protests to himself as he sets about his task. "And why does she have to threaten to smack me before I've done anything? Is it fair? Is it kind?"

"Ho," he tells himself, "if a person begins to think about things that are unfair or unkind . . ."

And then he begins to think.

He thinks of the time when he visited the house of his closest friend and watched his friend's father, a *shochet,* slit the throat of a chicken casually, cold-bloodedly, without a tremor of compunction.

"Pinele," he had said to his friend, "your father is an *epikoros,* a heathen."

"And why is my father an *epikoros?*"

"Because he has no pity for the living. He killed that chicken and didn't even feel sorry for it."

After which a quarrel had ensued and now the little boy and Pinele are friends no more.

Or of the time when the cook beat the cat for stealing a chicken liver from the salting board and then counted up the chickens again to discover that all the livers were present and accounted for. Whereupon the little boy informed her that she owed the cat an apology for having beaten it unjustly. At which the exasperated cook had slapped his face and thrown him out of the kitchen.

Or of the time when the dog had got scalded and the little boy had chased after it to comfort it, and his father had come upon him running after the dog, had accused him of being a dog beater, and had dragged him off to *cheder* by the ear.

Or of the time, on a Sabbath afternoon, when, dressed in his *Shabbos* best, he had wandered into the woods and come upon two peasant boys who had found a nest with fledgling birds, and were beating them to death one after the other against a tree trunk, and he had not been able to stand it, and had tried to stop them, only to get set upon for his pains, to return home to another spanking at his father's hands for fighting and getting his *Shabbos* suit torn.

"I don't understand it," the child reasons to himself, "the rebbe in *cheder* says that one mustn't harm a single living thing, not a fly or an ant, not even a spider. For these too are God's creatures. And these too suffer when they are hurt. Then if that's so, why do people beat dogs and cats, and kill birds and slaughter chickens? And not birds and cows and chickens only!"

What about Perelle, the paralyzed baby girl from the house next door whom he used to carry about on pleasant days so that she might sit in the sunlight, and who, whenever he lifted her, twined her thin arms tight about his neck, for she loved him dearly as he loved her. When the pogrom broke out, didn't men throw her out of the window so that her crippled body lay broken, bleeding, dead in the courtyard? And doesn't Perelle's mother cry all the time? And doesn't his own mother say to her, "*Sha,* you mustn't cry. It was God's will, you mustn't sin"?

Thinking of this, the little boy begins to cry himself, his tears streaming down his face.

"You little fool," his mother snaps at him, "I told you to remember to keep your eyes shut."

And she slaps him for being stupid.

A touching story, even in this condensed and mutilated form. But it is more than merely a touching story. It is a profound and wise one as well. For at one and the same time it bespeaks three things: a hard, tragic fact of life;

a moral inference from that fact; and finally a bright, a wonderful miracle.

The hard tragic fact is that of the universality of suffering, the truth that to live is to suffer, whether one be the little boy, or Perelle, or Perelle's mother, or the chicken beating out its lifeblood, or the cat eluding the broom, or the ant crushed beneath a human foot.

All life is a great fellowship of anguish in which each of us participates in some fashion or other. One of us suffers pains of the body; another terrors of the mind, the fear of insanity, or agonies of inferiority and insecurity. The heart of a third aches with loneliness, friendlessness, lovelessness. A fourth is tormented by remorse for old mistakes, errors, sins. Yet one more eats himself alive with jealousy and malice. Still another is haunted by a sense of pointlessness, being one of those multitudes who, as Thoreau put it, "live out lives of quiet desperation."

"The heart knows its own bitterness," the Scripture tells us; every man inhabits his own private Hell, or multiplicity and variety of Hells. That is the hard, tragic fact in Sholom Aleichem's story, the actuality of *Weltschmerz*, of the *tzar baale chayim*, the anguish of all that lives.

And the moral inference is a simple, natural deduction from the tragic fact: the thesis that since all things suffer, all things merit our pity.

This is the premise behind Sholom Aleichem's story, and this is the great foundation stone of all Jewish ethics: that a man must have mercy on everyone and everything; to be pitiless is a grave sin, perhaps the gravest of which man is capable.

Where, in Judaism, is this principle not expressed!
The Bible asserts it again and again:

"Thou shalt not oppress the stranger, for thou knowest the soul of the stranger, seeing you were strangers in the land of Egypt." Alas for strangers in an alien land!

"Thou shalt not curse the deaf nor put a stumbling block before the blind." Alas for him who cannot hear, alas also for him who cannot see!

"Thou shalt not muzzle thine ox when he threshes thy grain." Alas for the poor beast!

"Who will inherit the bliss of Paradise," a rabbi was once asked by his disciples. And in answer he pointed not to scholars, or to men of piety, but to two comedians playing in the market place. "But why?" his disciples cried in perplexity. "Because," he said, "they are men of mercy. I have noticed that when they see sad persons among their spectators, they make special efforts to be amusing and to lighten the heavy heart."

And that haunting last phrase in the book of Jonah, its concluding words, "not to mention the many cattle"— the phrase spoken by God when Jonah implores him to destroy Nineveh so that his, Jonah's, reputation as a Prophet may not be impaired, and God answers:

"And shall I not have pity on Nineveh that great city, wherein are so many people that cannot distinguish between their right hand and their left, not to mention the many cattle?"

Indeed the very God-faith in Judaism is sometimes, as in the case of the prophet Hosea, an expression of pity, an expression of the demand that since the volume of misery is so vast in the world there shall be in it a Being capable of equal and balancing compassion.

But if all this be true, then Judaism supplies us with a supreme criterion for judging ourselves and others.

He is a failure as a human being, no matter what his other traits and achievements, whose heart does not hurt for his fellow man. And he is a successful human being, no matter where else he may be lacking, who is rich in compassion.

Do not tell me of some financier, industrialist, merchant prince, or lawyer, how ingenious and capable he is, how great an enterprise he has established, how broad the influence he exerts, how vast the wealth he commands. Tell me this first: does he lord it over those who come to him for business favors, making them eat crow? Does he despise those who are less successful than he? When in conformity with the wolf-pack law of modern business he gains some victory over his competitors, what is his mood? Is there or is there not in him a twinge of regret, a spasm of sympathy for the one to whom his own triumph spells defeat?

Tell me this first: how does he treat his help: his aging and no longer too competent bookkeeper who will have difficulty finding other employment, his unorganized employees who have no union to protect them?

Tell me these things and I know the essentials about him, that to which everything else is secondary.

What is true for personal relations is equally true for things of the mind. I would not always have said this. There was a time, and that not so long ago, when I was so bedazzled by intellectual attainments that I rated man's head higher than his heart, the philosopher above the saint. In those days, the person I admired most in all the world was a professor, a man of staggering erudition, vast profundity, dazzling brilliance. To know what he knew, to think thoughts as deep and creative as his, to be capable of his felicity of expression: this was my highest aspiration.

It did not seem important to me then that he was cruel in debate, not only with his colleagues who were presumably his equals, but also with his students. What was it to me that it was his pleasure to demolish students with crushing remarks, or that he was not above baiting some slow-witted youngster into tearful confusion? He was learned, he was brilliant. And that was all that mattered.

It does not seem so to me today. I still revere a great mind, but I revere a great heart more. In part because, like everyone else of our generation, I have discovered of what monstrosities the merciless intellect is capable. In even greater part because having grown older I am less of a Hellenist than I used to be and more of a Jew. I understand of late what Heine meant when he said that the Greeks of the Periclean Age, for all their dazzling attainments, were only striplings, whereas the Hebrews were mature men. For a Jew, if he be truly a Jew, is compassionate. But compassion consists in an awakened and mature heart. And an awakened, mature heart comes only with time.

There is a sad joke or anecdote that came out of Germany a few years ago, the wry story of two little girls, both supposedly Aryans, who told each other in a moment of confidence that each had an aged grandparent who was a Jew. After reflecting a moment on their mutual disclosures, one of the little girls declared:

"Do you know what it must be? That's what must happen to people when they get old, they turn into Jews."

Now, too, we can see why Judaism opposes, why it must oppose, the two destructive social philosophies of our age. Judaism opposes fascism, the totalitarianism of the right, because fascism is concerned with neither justice nor mercy, but only power and the security of wealth. Judaism must oppose orthodox Marxism also, because though it is dedicated to social justice, genuinely dedicated, I believe, it is ready to sacrifice mercy to attain it.

For this is an integral part of the Communist program, that compassion must be suspended for a time—not permanently, but just long enough to get the social revolution launched, or to avert counterrevolution. In the end, the comrades promise, they will give us a society which is not only just, but merciful also, with the state and all forms of coercion melted away in the fully equitable humane classless society. Just let us be ruthless for a little while, they urge, it's in a good cause.

Do not believe it, not even for a moment, says the Jewish tradition, either in connection with communism or any other cause. Cruelty is not a cloak to be donned and doffed at will. It grows on its practitioners until it is a fixed habit. It corrupts their souls, perverts their purposes, ending only in evil. Most decisive, Judaism says of all such counsels that they overlook the crucial fact about

man: that man is always pitiable, even man the capital-
ist, the Trotskyite, the Kulak. Therefore there is not time
or occasion on which we are free not to pity him.

But that bright miracle in connection with pity, the
third of its features—what is that?

I suppose there is not an aspect of life which, if seen
afresh, is not a marvel, from the taste of bread on the
palate to the song of a bird at sunrise, to the bird itself
and the sunrise itself, and the bread and the palate. But
of all such marvels pity, it seems to me, is among the
greatest, the least explainable, the most nearly impossible.

Consider for a moment what incredible things occur
when we pity one another.

There are you, here am I, each encased in his own skin,
locked up in his own skull, separated by space, isolated
units of consciousness.

Self-contained, we are also self-centered. So far as each
of us is concerned, the entire universe revolves around him.
To preserve my life I may do the most desperate and
shameful things, and not for my life alone—for my comfort, my wealth, my pride, my prestige.

What is more, we are so made that we shrink from
pain, avoid it whenever we can, certainly never seek it out.
There is a certain quota of suffering of his own which each
of us has to endure. Is not that enough, we tell ourselves,
that we should go borrowing the pain of others?

And yet, incredible miracle that it be, this is just what
we do when we pity one another, we get out of ourselves,

into someone else, and by our own free will, accept his pain as our own.

Is there in all the world a more amazing, paradoxical phenomenon than this, or one more happily wonderful?

Unfortunately the whole process is so swift, pity goes from us to others or from others to us with such lightning speed that, whether we be the pitiers or the pitied, we are left not quite sure as to exactly what has happened. But this is too precious an event to go un-understood. Let us then retard the camera so that we may see the marvelous occurrence in slow motion. Let us insist that the magician in us, the prestidigitator of the spirit, repeat his sleight of hand step by step so that we may observe how his trick is done.

What happens to us, in us, when we pity?

Always three, and sometimes four events.

First of all, there is a flight of the imagination. We get out of the prison of ourselves, hurl ourselves through space into the inside of the little boy of Sholom Aleichem's story, as the little boy has put himself into the cat or little Perelle. In this respect, the act of pity is closely akin to artistic insight, to the vision into others of the portrait painter or novelist.

After the flight of the imagination, along with it, goes identification. We become one with the little boy, sharing his bruised bewilderment, as he has made himself one with the chicken whose throat is being slit or Perelle falling to her death.

Then occurs the third step, which is approbation. We have to like and approve before we can pity. We have to

approve of the person we pity, we have to approve of ourselves, for in pity we and the other become one, and if we
dislike either, we will dislike both. To take an extreme instance, consider the sadist, the pervert who takes pleasure
in the pain of others. He executes the first two steps: imagination, identification. But he is incapable of the third,
approbation. Hating himself, he hates the person with
whom he identifies himself. The sufferings of that person
evoke in him not pity, but pleasure. For through these
sufferings he is punishing himself.

There is still a fourth step, which may or may not be
taken, and which determines whether pity, which is
straight emotion, is to become mercy, an ethical ideal.

Pity, like love, is a feeling. It may be wise or unwise,
worthy or unworthy. One may pity wrongly, stupidly,
even corruptly.

Self-pity is a case in point—to be unjustifiably sorry
for poor me. Mercy, however, as opposed to pity, is thought
as well as feeling. It is pity checked against and controlled
by the requirements of morality, especially of justice. It is
pity transmuted into a conscious ethical principle.

It always remains true that justice must be done, but
mercy is no antagonist to justice. It should attend it. Let
justice be done, says Judaism. But let it be done merci-
fully, so that the justice dispensed is not vengeful or mechanical, but such as is dispensed by an understanding
judge, or by a father when he chastises his child. It is
tempered by love and understanding.

Now we see why mercy is a sign, not of weakness, as
Nietzsche argued, and the Nazis after him, but of strength.

A stupid person cannot pity; he lacks the required imagination. The immature person, the narcissist who has never outgrown his infantile self-centeredness, cannot pity because he is unable to concern himself with anyone else.

The morbid soul, the person who hates himself, cannot pity because the effect of his identification with others is that he comes to hate them also.

And the immoralist may be capable of instinctive pity but not of conscious mercy, for he lacks standards of justice through which one is elevated into the other.

The truth is that only a healthy soul is capable of pity, and a strong mind of mercy.

The incapacity for pity is a terrible, a loathsome disease. But there is something even more terrible, and that is willful pitilessness. I am speaking of the people—and their name is legion—in whom the power of compassion is present but who suppress it, deliberately, cold-bloodedly; who say: "Do not tell us, we do not wish to hear. Do not show us, we do not wish to see." And if by some chance they should see, and hear, against their will, they harden their hearts and refuse to let them be moved.

This is not a new sin. The ancient rabbis knew it and had a name for it. They called it *kashuv rach'mim,* the suppression of mercy. In the *al Het,* the great confession, it is the second sin listed—the hardening of the heart. It is not a new sin, but I doubt whether ever before in history there has been so much of it in the world: a thousand evidences around us testify how widespread, how deep-seated in men these days is this sin of willful pitilessness.

It must be checked or it will destroy us. It will spread among us, grow in us, making us capable of ever greater brutalities, until in the end we become totally dehumanized and our world perishes. For without mercy as without justice, mankind cannot endure.

There is no other way: men must stop hating and begin to pity. And the proper place for them to start is with and inside themselves.

Let us then begin by returning to compassion, even if we are alone in the world in doing so. In the first place we are Jews, and Jews have always boasted that they are *rachmanim bnei rachmanim,* compassionate sons of compassionate fathers. Let us make good on that boast.

This then is our sole, our ultimate chance, that by beginning to pity once more we may start a chain reaction of compassion, a contagion of it, leaping from heart to heart until all the world is alive with it once more.

Or to change the metaphor, who knows? Perhaps if enough of us distill out of our own hearts enough drops of mercy, such a tide of it will well forth from all of us together as to refloat the human ship and bring it safely home.

And suppose not? Suppose that because of our sins and stupidities it is fated that the human enterprise go down in flaming ruins, and we with it. If this is the case, can we have any better rule than compassion? Then, if we perish, it will yet be in a manner truly human and with whatever mutual solace we may have to afford one another.

Come weal, come woe, let us pity the living, all the

living. Let us approach each other with especial gentleness, husbands and wives, parents and children, friends, man to man, man to the beast of the field and fowl of the air, even the creeping things of the earth, as friends about to embark on a high but perilous enterprise might link arms on setting forth, or as a child about to enter a dark chamber might reach out for his mother's hand.

CHAPTER 15

THE DEPTH OF EVIL

IN THIS season of confession which culminates with the Day of Atonement, I have a special confession to make, and it is this: until recently I did not subscribe to what is after all the main motif of our Yom Kippur ritual—its insistence on the deep sinfulness of human nature.

That familiarity breeds contempt is an old truth. But it breeds blindness, too. Just because we know the Yom Kippur prayer book so well, we are likely to miss its central thesis. Let us turn its pages once again, and this time mark critically what it is saying.

On the very first page is the *Kol Nidre,* a liturgy based on the premise that try as men will to do the good, they must fail in some measure, wherefore each of them needs absolution.

Let us reflect on the following passages:

"Aye it is thus, evil hath us in bond."

"Look, God, to Thy covenant, and not to our evil inclination."

"What is our piety, what our righteousness?"

"Are we not vessels filled with shame and confusion?"

243

"Do thou subdue our evil impulses."

"Circumcise our hearts."

Besides these, the Lesser Confession is recited ten times during Yom Kippur, the Greater Confession nine times.

What is the point of all this? What except that man is inevitably sinful, that the evil in his nature runs fierce and deep.

But perhaps this thesis of the depth of evil in man is limited to the Yom Kippur prayer book. Perhaps in its eagerness to move men to penitence, Judaism on this occasion indulges in exaggeration, in dramatic overstatement. Perhaps Judaism normally takes a brighter view of man's character.

There was a time when I used to tell myself this.

It is simply not true.

What the Yom Kippur prayer book asserts is asserted by all of historical Judaism.

Consider the Bible. What are its best known and best loved stories? They are:

Of Adam and Eve who had only one commandment to
    observe, but being perverse could not observe
    even that one;

Of Cain who with a whole world to divide with Abel,
    still envied his brother's portion and so came
    to murder him;

Of men who by their wickedness brought on a
    deluge;

Of a generation of the desert, who called to be
    a Kingdom of Priests and a Holy Nation, still

244

preferred slavery in Egypt so long as fleshpots went with it.

What does the Bible assume in all these tales except that men are sinful and that deeply rooted is evil in them? And lest anyone misunderstand, the Bible makes the point explicitly and often:

> For the inclination of man's heart
> is evil from his youth.

> Crooked is the heart above all things,
> and desperately weak.

What the Bible teaches, the rabbis teach also. Anyone who knows the Talmud, Midrash, and later rabbinic works knows also their doctrine of the split in man between the *Yetzer Tov,* the good inclination, and the *Yetzer ha-Ra,* the evil inclination.

It cannot be gainsaid: Judaism's judgment of man is somber.

Somber, yes! Pessimistic, no! But how can this be? Can any opinion of man be more melancholy than the one we have just reviewed?

Observe Christianity for an answer to that question!

Christianity teaches the doctrine of original sin, the belief introduced by Paul that every person is tainted with Adam's sin, is a sinner at birth and so is damned even before he has begun to live.

Christianity teaches further the total depravity of man, that man is not only sinner but a hopeless sinner to boot, that nothing in him or in his actions is free from evil.

And in conclusion, it teaches the powerlessness of man to achieve goodness, his impotence to win salvation except as a gift of God's grace.

With such deeply pessimistic notions, Judaism has no sympathy.

If it calls man a sinner, it also calls him "little lower than the angels." If it describes him as capable of abysmal evil it insists that he is equally capable of dazzling good. It holds that he is born not predamned but with a clean slate; that he has the power to keep himself righteous, or, having erred, to recapture his righteousness; that his salvation is up to him.

Compared to Christianity, Judaism is wildly optimistic about man.

And yet, though more cheerful than the Christian doctrine, the Jewish remains somber enough. Man is still, in its judgment, a creature easily liable to sin, with evil implanted deep within him.

It is this notion—that man is sinful and that evil inheres in him—which I used to be unable to accept.

For I am a child of my generation, a creature of the twentieth century—a modern man. And if there is anything which characterizes the modern man it is his optimism in general and his boundless optimism concerning human nature in particular.

The modern man believes two things about man.

First that whatever evil is in him is superficial, something induced not something inherent; second, since all human evil is induced, it can be eliminated or corrected by eliminating or correcting the circumstances which have induced the evil.

Let me be more concrete. The modern man assumes that whenever anything goes wrong with a human being, something has gone wrong with his circumstances. Perhaps he has not been fed well enough, or his parents did not understand him as a child, or he was exposed to faulty education, or he had to live in a slum, or he could not find a job, or he made the wrong marriage.

Always something outside man is responsible for whatever goes awry within him. Never is it suggested that the fault may lie on the inside.

What then is the inference?

It is this: if only we can give every child an adequate diet, understanding parents, proper education, sanitary housing, and economic security, every man will be well behaved and virtuous. Evil in man will be no more.

I will not enter here into the history of this brightly optimistic notion of human nature; I will not demonstrate, as I believe I could, that it is really modern, that neither the ancient nor medieval world knew it, that it was born only with the renaissance; that it is a natural consequence of the expansion of scientific knowledge and of man's mastery over nature; nor will I try to show here how much of the modern temper this notion explains— its experimentalism, its restless search for new ideas and techniques—yes, even its faddism. I shall confine myself to considering the two views of man: the somber view of Judaism, the bright view of modernity.

Into this modern view I was born, inhaling it almost

with my first breath. Certainly I was educated in it. Accepting it, I have always resented the other less cheerful outlook exemplified in our Yom Kippur *Mahzor*.

But I have grown older and I hope wiser. I no longer am so optimistic as I once was about human nature. Slowly but steadily, I have moved from the modern doctrine of man to the Jewish.

What induced this change in me?

There was, first of all, the stand taken by Judaism. I have a very healthy respect for the Jewish tradition; it is so consistently sound on the basic issues of living. If then it took a particular position on man, then I was inclined to feel that there must be something to it—all the more because in other respects Judaism holds so high an opinion of human nature. Hence, even when I was most completely a child of the modern world, I could not help remembering Judaism's dissent. It troubled me much as, I suppose, a general practitioner of medicine is troubled to find a distinguished specialist disagreeing with his diagnosis.

No doubt, too, I was influenced by the new psychiatry—by the knowledge recently won that at the core of the human personality is a complex of blind, irrational drives which Freud and his successors have shown to be stubborn and persistent, ruthless and tyrannical, devious and wily. They can be tamed and controlled. They are unmoral rather than immoral. They are capable of being turned to the good, but also of being blinded to evil.

Then, too, I have grown suspicious over the fact that all the measures taken to reform man have reformed him so little. I can think of dozens of proposals each of which, according to its proponents, would turn men into angels, and society into a paradise. Such claims were made on behalf of political democracy, woman suffrage, universal popular education, social insurance, progressive education, *laissez faire* capitalism, socialism, communism, psychoanalysis, semantics, and what not else. Of these reforms many have been achieved: women can vote; everyone is not only free to attend school, but is required to do so; progressive methods have been introduced into pedagogy; some people have been psychoanalyzed; Russia is in a fashion a Socialist society—and still men, including Russians, continue to be about as selfish and cruel as ever, and their society as unstable and unjust.

I do not wish to be misunderstood; I am not deprecating social reform. I believe in it as passionately as ever. I know that much of the evil in men is made, encouraged, and intensified by their society. I treasure and will fight for every bit of additional freedom, justice, mercy, security, and peace that can be injected into human affairs. All I am doing now is looking a fact in the face—the distressing fact that all the reforms have accomplished less than had been hoped, not because the reforms were ill advised, but because the Old Adam is deeper in us than, in our optimism, we had supposed.

And so I have been swung around from my old modern optimism, first by the historic Jewish position; second by the new psychiatry; third by recent history; and fourth by the unsatisfactory results of social reform. But most of all I have been won over by an accumulation of everyday experience.

I remember once, how, as a graduate student of philosophy at Columbia University, I chanced to enter the subway in the company of one of my professors. The man was, needless to say, highly educated. He was in good health, happily married, and generally well adjusted. He was the epitome of the civilized decent modern man. Yet when we stood in the crowded train, and someone jostled him, he became a near beast before my eyes. The first time he was jostled he pulled away irritably from the man next to him. The second time he turned and glared at the inadvertent and unwitting offender. The third time his face paled, his hands clenched, his breath came faster, he could barely keep from snarling and striking out.

So irritable are we, even the most civilized. So near to the surface is the animal in all of us, the impulse of hostility and aggression.

Or consider a more general experience which every one of us has shared. How often have we discussed some topic with friends—a topic perhaps of no interest to us at all —only to find ourselves arguing passionately, angrily, cruelly.

What is the meaning of these commonplace and disagreeable incidents? Our pride has been awakened—our love of self. We have identified ourselves with our point of view. If we can establish it, we shall be showing how bright we are. On the other hand every criticism of it becomes a criticism of us. If it should be refuted, we shall be humiliated. And so we argue not for the sake of truth, not to persuade others, but to protect our prestige.

A trivial illustration, it may seem, but most revealing of the power of pride in human affairs, of its capacity to corrupt even the best men and the highest ideals. One detects it not only in vain persons and empty pursuits, but in scientists, economists, theologians, all of whom argue for their theories in part for the truth's sake, but in part also out of self-love.

And again we make a mistake, most of us, when we think of evil only in its grosser aspects, in terms of stupidity, murder, theft, alcoholism, or as the affliction only of base people, criminal or near criminal. The domain of evil is far more universal. It reaches into all of us, into the best of us and into the best areas of our beings. When man is at his highest he is still a creature irritable and aggressive, proud and vain, selfish and self-deluding.

But what is the relevance of this point? Suppose it is true, as it seems to be, that evil is deep and intense in man. It is a melancholy and depressing truth; it is something we should not dwell on, least of all in our religious meditations.

It is not my purpose to dishearten anyone. Nor am I happy that the truth I am expounding is disagreeable. But it is the truth and like every other truth cannot be ignored.

Naïve optimism concerning man is of course more pleasant, but like all illusions it is very dangerous.

First of all, it invites its opposite—disillusion. Anyone who elects to live in a fool's paradise is asking for trouble. Sooner or later the truth must break through, and when it dawns he is unprepared for it, may even be demoralized by it. This holds of all illusions; it holds therefore of illusions about men. How many disillusioned people we meet nowadays, people soured on human nature. They expected too much from it. I myself know scores such. Let me refer to one class only: tired liberals who expected utopia to be ushered in if only the proper law was enacted or the right person elected. The law was enacted, the person was elected and utopia still has not arrived. So they are through with human progress. You know the breed, the ex-radical turned reactionary, the ex-reformer who sneers at all ideals—men ruined by excessive optimism, by their naïveté and illusions.

The fact of the matter is that evil is within man as well as outside him—and we shall have to recognize this truth if we are ever to get anywhere. Otherwise we will forever be failing to do our first duty, which is to go to work on ourselves. A man, say the rabbis, must always "speak the truth in his own heart." For if he does not, if he conceals from himself the presence in his soul, and in the souls of other men also, of aggression, pride, and selfishness, he will forever be busy doing all things except that which needs to be done first and most urgently—attending to souls, his own and those of other men.

At all costs then—the truth, no matter how grim and discouraging.

But *is* the truth so grim and discouraging?

To be sure it is not as pleasant as we should like, as in our naive optimism we are accustomed to believe. But there is nothing in it to discourage us.

"Look you to the rock whence ye were hewn—to the prophets, rabbis and sages of Israel."

They knew the truth, they proclaimed it openly in the Bible, the Talmud, the prayer book. They knew the truth and were not a jot disheartened by it. Why then need we be discouraged, we who have at our disposal the new psychology with its insights into the workings of the human personality, not to speak of our mastery over nature and social processes. If they could be of good cheer, we certainly can.

Let us note further what the sages of Israel never forgot—that if man's evil is very deep, his goodness can also be very high. If men can stoop to any meanness, and justify themselves in it, they are also capable of staggering heroism. If they are often quickly irritable, they are as often infinitely gentle and patient. Men can be humble as well as vain. They cannot only forget their selfish interests, they can and often do sacrifice them.

Let us recall too the Jewish teaching that the evil in man, no matter how deep and persistent, can be tamed. Tough and resistant as it is, it can be controlled. Perhaps it cannot be eliminated altogether; it can certainly be reduced in bulk and influence.

In sum, let us go forth to the good fight with high hearts. The fight is more protracted and difficult than we would like to think. It is not only not hopeless, it can be won. Not that evil can quickly or easily be subdued. Not that it can be altogether destroyed. The victory over it will never be final or total. But why should we be superior to partial victories?

CHAPTER 16

FROM THE MOUNTAINTOPS

I WILL lift mine eyes unto the mountains whence cometh my help."

It is a curious fact that in the mystic speculation of all religions, and especially of Judaism, the hills and mountains seem to occupy a unique and unusual place. When Abraham is commanded to sacrifice his son, God bids him take the lad to Mount Moriah and offer him up "on one of the hills which I shall show thee." When God would give Israel the Torah, the Law of Life, the body of eternal verities, the place of revelation again is signified as the top of a mountain. Before Moses dies, he asks to see the Land of Promise, and he is ordered to climb to the top of Mount Nebo. When Elijah demands that Israel choose between Jehovah and Baal, he summons the idolatrous priests to the top of Mount Carmel for the final and critical test; and the psalmist looking for God's help raises his eyes to the mountains apparently with the feeling that on the high places of the earth he is somehow nearer the divine.

In all of these instances it appears as though our ancestors had the feeling that there was something mysterious about the mountains and the hilltops; that they somehow furnish man with a clairvoyance which he does not normally possess. It is as though they felt that one could see from the hills what one could not see in the valley or the plain.

It is not hard to understand this intuition. One does see from the mountains what one cannot see from the depths. One sees more clearly and further, and one sees the whole landscape and not merely a part of it.

Recently I came across a biography, *Escape from the Soviets,* in which the author describes a dramatic experience. A father, mother, and child are fleeing from a Communist prison. They are fighting their way through the deep woods that straddle the border of Russia and Finland. Their supplies are gone, their compass is lost, and they find themselves completely bewildered in the woods. Panic overtakes them; and when they discover that they have been moving in a circle, that after two days of fighting their way through tangled underbrush, they have returned to the spot which they thought they had left far behind them, the three trapped and lost human beings sit themselves down, too sick at heart even for tears. In an apathetic despair they await death from starvation. Suddenly it occurs to them that from the hill one can see what is hidden in the valley. With failing strength they climb the nearest summit, and there before them spreads the whole terrain. There is sunlight where in the woods there was only shadow. The streams which wound in tangles across their path now flow in general directions from them, they have a picture of the lie of the land.

As they discover where they are, as they learn once more what is north, what is south, east, and west, their despair slips from them and they set off boldly for their haven.

I recall this simple story because it is a concrete and vivid illustration of the truth which our ancestors felt vaguely when they associated great acts with high mountains. For in life, too, we get lost. We find ourselves in a jungle of emotions, baffled in an underbrush of problems, moving without light and without direction. In life, too, we fail to see the forest for the trees. And just as these refugees from Russia climbed a hilltop to recover direction, purpose, and courage, so we too, lost human souls in the wilderness of life, need mountaintops if we are to recover our perspective.

Occasionally, then, we must abandon our trodden path, our routines and our disciplines, our individual problems and concerns. Occasionally we must climb above the jungles that hem us in if we are to be able to discover in which direction we are going, and how much progress we have made.

And herein lies the importance of Rosh Hashanah and Yom Kippur. These days are, as it were, mountaintops of the spirit from which we can catch glimpses of the whole of life. During the other days of the year our lives are so lost in the forest of living that we see neither the whole of reality nor its general pattern. But on these days we start apart from and above our normal lives; we perceive not only the pieces of the puzzle, but the whole pattern.

Let us consider ourselves, assembled here in the synagogue, and our lives. There is not a person here who has not, in the course of this Rosh Hashanah morning, thought of his own problems and perplexities. One may have been overwhelmed by concern for his material welfare, over that wealth which was his security against the future. Another sits here whose life has been embittered by unfortunate personal relations. Even those of us who have been relatively fortunate, who are still secure economically, who have experienced no great sorrow and no great loss, whose hearts have not been bruised—even we have been perplexed and saddened. For it is not only our individual problems which oppress us at this moment. A vague, poignant pathos afflicts us. . . . Another year gone its way. What a solemn thought that must be to us who have so brief a span of sunlight between the dawn and the dusk. Life is speeding on. Soon another year, and another, and another—each filled with its emotions and sorrows. And then all too soon, the twilight.

When we consider how our days have been spent, and how soon they shall be ended, we ask ourselves, "What does it all mean—this strange business of living?" And we cannot help but be touched by a sickening sense that it may have no meaning at all: that all this business of birth, suffering, and death, that all these are but the proverbial tale of an idiot, full of sound and fury, signifying nothing.

Such is life as seen from the valley, through the underbrush—pointless, planless, irrational.

But on this day we are bidden to climb the mountains. And when we stand on high, apart from ourselves, we discover that our troubles do not loom so large. As the swamp through which the lost traveler struggled for hours is only a little pool when seen from the hills, so when we view the whole of our lives we see that yesterday's difficulties in business and last week's quarrel with our friend are, after all, not quite as important as we imagined when we stood face to face with them. We learn that our great anxieties were so great because we stood too close to them. Viewing our whole lives, we recall that last year and the year before we also had our pains and aches, our desires and frustrations, that they passed away and that they no longer hurt us. And we take courage in the thought that the immediate problem before us will also pass away and that someday we shall look back to that, too, and say, as an ancient Roman poet said: *"et haec olim meminisse iuvabit."*

So also with our sense of meaninglessness and frustration. Stand close to an oil painting, and what do you see? Only a confusion of daubs of paint. Do you wish to see the design and pattern? Stand back, then, and witness a miracle. For as you withdraw from the painting, the strokes begin to fit together, the individual daubs take on relationship to one another, take on meaning collectively: all unite to form a pattern and design. So in this business of living we lose the pattern because we stand too close.

And the things which we fear most, the great calamities of life, even they, somehow or other, seen in their proper perspective, are not so fearful. We are all afraid of pain, we shudder away from the necessity of struggle, and we all recoil from death. But if we climb high enough even these horrors somehow fit into the pattern. Pain and struggle, the terrors of living, we see as the principles of growth and of sympathy. If there were no struggle, man would never have risen beyond the animal. It is the need for struggle that has compelled him to move. And if there were no pain man would have no compassion and no love. Death itself, that grim specter—even that fits into our view of the whole. For we see it from the mountain no longer as a personal enemy, but as the great releaser. When life has been lived long enough, death steps in. And when our generation has scrawled the slate so badly that it needs erasing, death removes that generation, so that a new generation may arise and start once again.

Thus does the view from the mountaintop liberate us from our individual troubles. Thus does it supply us with a sense of meaning.

Thus he who stands on the mountaintop may be moved with new courage and determination. But he must also be touched with a sense of his own smallness. It is only in the valley that man becomes proud; only there he occupies so large a place in what he sees, that he is deluded into a sense of his importance. The hills teach us humility. And in the words of Carlyle we say to ourselves, "Little man, why so hot?"

But much as we require a mountain view if we are to see our own lives as a whole, infinitely more do we require it when we judge our fellow man. We read in Scripture about Balaam who was hired to curse Israel. He traveled many miles to earn the reward promised him for the right kind of curse. The time came for him to pronounce it, and he climbed the mountain to look upon those he was to curse. And there he discovered that he was unable to curse; he could only bless.

At this moment there may come to your mind the recollection of a wrong someone inflicted on you, the slander someone spread about you, the humiliation someone visited on you; and thinking of it, you may be sick all over again. Viewing your wrong at close range you resent, you hate, you condemn. But from the mountaintop it all takes on a different perspective. You see not a part of the personality which you despise, but the whole of it. You discover that to do wrong is as natural as to live, that all men hurt their fellows, even when they love them. Once we stand apart from ourselves, we see that we, too, have slandered and wounded. We have been wronged; but on high we are reminded that we, too, have wronged.

And seeing from the hilltop the whole personality of him who has hurt us, we see that he too is but a product of his background and education, that he, too, is a lost soul struggling to make his way in a world of difficulties. If he has wronged, it is because something in his heredity, his environment, or his immediate circumstances drove him to it. We see the poor, twisted, distorted life of the man who hurt us—so much like our own. And having seen the unity of all human beings from the hills, having caught the perspective of the whole of our fellow man, and not merely that part of him which offended us, it is no longer possible for us to hate him. We understand, we sympathize, and we forgive.

It is the purpose of religion to help us see life from a high place, so that we can see it steadily and see it whole. It is the function of religion to take us, prisoners trapped in the lowlands, bewildered in the forest, floundering in the swamps, and lead us to the hills, from which we can contemplate the whole. Centuries ago the Psalmist said, "I will lift mine eyes unto the mountains, whence cometh my help." Now perhaps we understand what he meant. Climb to the hilltops, and you will see a light which will illumine your steps as you make your pilgrimage through the forests of life.

CHAPTER 17

TELLING ONESELF THE TRUTH

꙾꙾꙾꙾꙾꙾꙾꙾꙾꙾꙾꙾꙾꙾꙾꙾꙾꙾꙾꙾꙾꙾꙾꙾꙾꙾꙾꙾꙾꙾꙾꙾꙾꙾꙾

N̲O PHRASE is more commonly used in connection with
Rosh Hashanah than the Hebrew words *heshbon
ha-nefesh*—a reckoning of the soul. It is part of this business of living that we develop comfortable habits of conduct. These we pursue from day to day until they hypno-
tize us and become a routine which we never attempt to
examine critically. But if our lives are ever to be better
than they have been, we must at times withdraw from
this daily repetition and look at it analytically. We must
stand for a moment outside of ourselves, and evaluate our
lives. Only then can we properly estimate our successes
and failures and undertake to remold the patterns of our
personality. It is for this reason that we observe Rosh
Hashanah—the days which the Jewish tradition has set
aside for this purpose.

And whenever I think of this as the day of the *heshbon
ha-nefesh*, I remember a passage which is to be found in
the prayer book, one which occurs so early in the service
that most of us have never seen it; yet one that throws a
clear light on this entire business of evaluating our lives.

The prayer quotes the sentiments of an early Midrash: "At all times let a man reverence God as much in private as in public, let him always acknowledge the truth and above all let him speak the truth in his own heart."

At first glance these words seem grotesque. We all know of the commandment to speak the truth to one another. That is a very simple and understandable moral precept to guide our relations with our fellow men. Had the prayer book said, "Speak the truth to your fellow," we would have understood at once; but what can this mean: "Speak the truth to yourself in your heart"?

How well these ancient rabbis knew human character, how deeply they understood the words of Jeremiah: "The heart is deceitful above all things, and it is desperately weak." How well they knew that just as men lie to themselves, just as they deceive their fellows, so they attempt to deceive their own hearts. Long before the modern psychologists, the rabbis had discovered that the greatest difficulty in the moral life of man is this pleasant trick that we all know, the art of self-deception, of lying to oneself. They illustrate this truth again and again. Does not the Bible tell us: "The lazy man says, there is a lion in the streets; if I go out I shall be slain"? Is not this the type of lying excuse with which a man unwilling to undertake a task apologizes to himself?

And when they warn us that one should tell himself the truth in his heart, they command us to resist a universal tendency—the tendency to manufacture a reason which is no reason in order to excuse ourselves from an act from which we cannot honestly be excused.

A hundred illustrations on the daily level spring to our minds, and show us how, in fact, the simplest among us are aware of the practice. For what else do we mean when we talk of somebody "kidding himself along"?

The man who has failed to effect an entrance into the group which he socially desires says, in his bitterness, "Oh, well, I'm too good for them." Or, "They're not in my class."

The husband or wife who has not had the patience or the skill to create the companionship which marriage should give, consoles himself with the lie: "She doesn't understand me," "He doesn't understand me."

The person of no culture who feels himself out of place at a gathering of educated and intelligent people, excuses himself with: "You can't butter your bread with books" or, "How does music help anyone make his living?"

And the man who has failed in business finds solace in the excuse that the breaks were against him, or, the boss had a grudge against him, or the firm didn't like Jews.

This tendency toward self-deception is exhibited also on the highest levels of the human intellect. When scientists and philosophers fool themselves, we do not say, as does the man in the street, that they are kidding themselves along; we use a much more dignified term; we say they are rationalizing. Thus a philosopher will decide what he wants to believe, and then go out and find the logic to prove it. Or a scientist will have some pet theory which he wants to demonstrate and then go out to look for the evidence, even to the extent of fabricating testimony.

There is unquestionably much more lying to oneself in the depths of the heart than there is to others. Because the lie which one tells oneself cannot be detected. There is no one who will challenge the falsehood which one speaks in the heart. And yet, self-deception is as dangerous as any other kind of deception. Like every lie it calls forth other lies to defend it, until out of the simplest falsehood has grown a cancerous tissue of other falsehoods. Moreover, so long as a man tells himself a lie about himself, he will do nothing to face the truth and correct it. The misunderstood husband, so long as he refuses to face the facts, will remain misunderstood; the incompetent employee will always find employers who have grudges against him; and the scientist will never discover the truth.

II

My purpose here and now, however, is not to develop a general moral truth; it is rather to give one definite, glaring, and dangerous illustration of it. For nowhere does one see more self-deception than that which we Jews practice on ourselves. Our lives as Jews are literally filled with lies that cripple us and keep us from doing our Jewish duty.

Jewish life is in process of disintegration; about it hangs a perceptible aura of corruption. The mind of the modern Jew is no longer Jewish. The dark ignorance of Jewish culture hangs like a pall everywhere. Never before in our history have Jews been so ignorant and so disinterested in Judaism or Jewish problems. For years I have watched Jewish homes grow less and less Jewish, seen custom after custom disappear, watched the Holidays recede into oblivion, the Sabbath lose its meaning. And my heart has grown sick—sick at the misfortune that has befallen us—at the ghastly, empty future that faces us.

And I have come to ask myself the "why" of all this. And now I feel that I know.

Is it that Judaism has no food for our souls, no beauty for our lives? Is it that we have honestly weighed Jewish tradition in the balance and found it wanting? Not at all. The real reason behind our failure as Jews is that we have lied to ourselves, that we have not spoken the truth in our hearts.

I say that we have deceived ourselves as Jews, that we have refused to look at the truth, and therefore we have permitted Jewish life to disintegrate before our eyes.

Each of us is aware of all this, and there come moments when we are troubled by what is happening to ourselves as Jews and what has befallen American Judaism generally. We feel, for an instant, that we ought to do something about it, that we ought to undertake to rededicate our lives, that we ought to try to restore a fuller and richer Jewish home. But then we take refuge in pleasant excuses that absolve us from responsibility. We tell ourselves that Judaism is inconvenient, that it is old-fashioned; we shrug our shoulders complainingly and protest, "What can I do about it?" or we console ourselves by saying, "That's not our problem, that's what rabbis are for, to worry about Judaism." Excuses, self-deceptions— lies in the heart and evasions of a problem. If we told ourselves the truth, we would recognize that basically the

266

problem is up to us as individuals, that Judaism stands or falls as each of us personally faces the situation. For Jewish life is made up of individual Jews. But to admit your responsibility means to assume an obligation and so you prefer to tell yourself pleasant lies that make no demands on you, and to shake your heads sadly at the collapse of Jewish life, and to blame for it the Rabbi, the Synagogue, Fate, Modern Times—anybody or anything except yourself.

III

There is not an American Jewish leader who has not stressed the importance of Jewish education. For we are a minority people, we can live only if we succeed in transmitting such knowledge and loyalty as will keep us from assimilation. The life of Israel depends on the Hebrew School. Nay, more, the happiness of the child and his success in life depends on just that. For your children will have to be Jewish whether they want to or not. And only a good Jewish education can guarantee that they will find pride and happiness in the Jewishness which is imposed upon them.

If our city were without Hebrew Schools, most of us could not rest or come to peace with our consciences until that lack were remedied. And yet, now that we have them, operating at minimum cost to the parents, our children get either no or an incomplete training in Hebrew culture. Why is it that we close the doors to a fuller Jewishness in the faces of our youth? Ask the typical parent and you will get any one of the following ridiculous answers: "My boy isn't going to be a rabbi." And yet the parent knows perfectly well that there are Jews who aren't rabbis, and that these Jews need Hebrew knowledge if they are to find richness in their Jewishness. Or again, "The poor child has not time to play." And this answer is advanced despite the fact that the child may be a picture of health; despite the fact that the mother will take time from the child's play for a piano lesson; despite the fact that the mother may realize that the child has too much time for play, and is constantly worried as to what the child is doing after school.

And actually, I have yet to learn of a case where any child's health has suffered because he attended Hebrew School sessions for one hour a day in clean, light, and airy classrooms. Have you ever heard that lame, old excuse, "My child isn't going to be Bar Mitzvah yet for a long time"? Or, "He has been Bar Mitzvah already"? Have you ever heard that ancient story about children coming home late from Hebrew School for dinner? And do you know that antique libel, "I've sent him to the Talmud Torah, but he doesn't learn anything"—as though any child can learn anything about any subject when the parents are indifferent or even hostile.

These are simply illustrations of this same tendency to deceive ourselves. The real reason is the fact that we have become such poor Jews, we have so completely lost sight of our obligations, that we don't really care. We are ashamed to admit our indifference, and so we advance these excuses to account for it.

Again, the real reason, fundamentally, is that guaranteeing a Hebrew education to a child means accepting some inconvenience; and so thin is our Jewish loyalty that we feel that it is not worth the sacrifice.

IV

The most flagrant example of Jewish self-deception is to be found in the Jewish home. We all appreciate and admire the Jewish home, with its poetry and beauty. We wax sentimental about that household which is Jewish from the *mezuzah* at the front door to the pots and pans in the kitchen. And when we picture to ourselves the peace of the Sabbath eve with the flickering candles, the blessing of children, the *Kiddush;* or when we recall the romantic symbolism of the *havdalah* at the departure of the Sabbath, we are overtaken by a sense of homesickness, a yearning for that soft loveliness which is Judaism in the home. We know then that we are not satisfied with the homes in which we live; they are only places where we eat and sleep, they have no romance, no beauty and no piety. We realize that when our children wander far from us in later years, they will have no soul-stirring memories to tie them to us.

Why are our homes like that? Why are there no Sabbath candles? No *Kiddush?* No *Havdalah?* No *Hanukkah?*

Oh, we have reasons, but they are reasons with which we lie to ourselves. We say all that is old-fashioned, it isn't being done any more. It's not modern. We tell ourselves that we don't get anything out of Jewish observance, without ever having tried it. The real reason is that it is slightly inconvenient. If there is to be *Kiddush,* the housewife must order her *challah,* must have candles lit, a wine cup must be ready, and the husband must make the supreme sacrifice of being home on time. Besides, we haven't done those things for so long that we should feel a bit awkward or ashamed before our own families if we began. And so, our homes are empty, cynical monuments to the fact that housewives won't take the trouble to telephone an order for a *challah,* so that children may have the Jewish poetry to which they are entitled.

V

And while I am on this subject, let me add something on the dietary laws. I know that these laws are in great disrepute. It is considered modern not to adhere to them. We have even come to the point of apologizing for observing them. We say that we maintain them for the sake of our parents or out of force of habit. But let's not deceive ourselves, and let no one minimize their importance. They help to keep us alive as a separate group. They discipline our characters. They make us self-conscious as Jews. No one who observes Jewish life will minimize their significance. A broad abyss separates the home in which they prevail from that from which they are absent. Is it an accident that where you find an intensely Jewish home you will find them observed? Is it an accident that intensely Jewish young people invariably come from homes which include this Jewish element too?

Of course, we have our reasons. We assure ourselves that we no longer need the dietary laws for our health. We insist that we don't see any point to them. Most ridiculously of all, we lay the blame on our maids. How, the housewife asks us, can you keep a kosher home with a maid in the kitchen? As though it is harder for a housewife to maintain *kashruth* when she has help than when she is without it. Our grandmothers, who did not know the luxury of a servant, did all their own housework, reared a large family all by themselves, and still managed to find time for a Jewish kitchen. And we who are liberated from all of that bondage can't find time to attend to this minor detail.

VI

There are times when the cause of Jewish life seems a desperate one, when it seems doomed to defeat. But I say that no battle is lost until the heart surrenders, no cause defeated until its adherents desert.

Judaism is not beaten yet, it has in the hearts of each Jew great untapped reservoirs of devotion. To these I appeal. Give a bit of yourselves to your people, make your lives more actively Jewish and, bit by bit, we shall wring victory from defeat, shall restore the fallen house of David. Bit by bit we shall win again that full richness of Jewish life which will mean beauty and peace for us, and light and blessing to our children to the end of all time.

CHAPTER 18

ON BEING THE VICTIM OF INJUSTICE

※※※※※※※※※※※※※※※※※※※※※※※※※※※※※※※※

HOW OUGHT a person to react when he is the victim of an injustice?

This is, I am frank to admit, a theoretical question. But rest assured that we shall, before we are through, find applications for the conclusions at which we arrive, applications sufficiently practical to suit the most hardheaded among us.

This then is our problem:

Suppose you have been wronged. How ought you to behave?

Suppose you have been wronged by one you imagined to be your true friend. Suppose you discover that he has been using you to his own purposes, or has slandered you behind your back, or made public property of your most intimate confidences. What should you feel, think, do?

Or suppose you have been injured in your business or profession, defrauded of your money, position, scientific discovery, your opportunities for advancement. What, in those circumstances, is the conduct proper to a human being?

In such situations, any one of three responses is possible: we can react as Machiavellians on the level of instinct, or according to Christian teaching, or according to Jewish.

Let us look at each of these in turn.

The instinctive response is not to be disposed of so lightly. It consists in the first impulse of any living creature, whether man or beast, on being hurt, which is to strike back, returning hurt for hurt and throwing in something extra for good measure, on the spot if possible but if not, then at the earliest propitious moment no matter how long it may be delayed. To get even, to take revenge, to exact an eye for an eye, a tooth for a tooth, this is the spontaneous impulse of both the savage and the most civilized of men.

It is not and has never been a Jewish doctrine. I go out of my way to say this so explicitly because the phrase "an eye for an eye" comes from the Torah and has been quoted by critics of Judaism as evidence that ours is a religion of vengefulness.

No greater misrepresentation is possible. At no time in Judaism was the commandment "an eye for an eye" applied literally by Jews. Always so far as we are aware it was interpreted to mean monetary restitution, the payment of damages for the injury inflicted. And as for Moses, his was a humane purpose when he put this injunction into the Torah. He was legislating against the practice common to all ancient systems of jurisprudence whereby under certain circumstances two eyes might be blinded for one, or the eyes of children for the offenses

273

of their fathers. Far from condoning savagery, he was protesting against disproportionate punishment.

This unavoidable parenthesis closed, we resume our argument to ask whether this is to be our course when we are the victims of injustice: To give measure for measure and something more?

Not if we are practical minded. For, by that something more which is an inevitable ingredient of revenge we throw the scales out of balance again, invite countermeasures to which we must respond once again, and so involve ourselves in an endless feud, a vicious cycle of retaliation.

Graver than the physical perils of this course are the spiritual perils. It leads to a fantastic self-centeredness, the aggrieved one almost always becomes so obsessed with the injury done him that he is left without a shred of mind or heart for anyone or anything else.

One thinks of Edmond Dantes in *The Count of Monte Cristo* or of Mr. Sedley in *Vanity Fair*—lives consumed by ancient wrongs. I know, as you know, of wives and husbands in broken marriages who, decades after the breach, still talk of nothing else than the injustice done them, who in consequence are burdens to their friends, and, by preventing themselves from making new lives, their own worst enemies.

The Christian ideal consists essentially in submission motivated by pity. Its classic instances is the saying of Jesus that if a man would take your cloak you shall give him your shirt also, and if he strike you upon one cheek then you must turn the other. There is a logic to this counsel. The man who demands your cloak may need it to protect himself against the cold; the person who slaps you may be driven to his act by some uncontrollable compulsion. In other words, he may be needy, or mad. But even if he is simply greedy or cruel, even then by not resisting you may shame him into decency. In any event, he is pitiable, and therefore to be indulged rather than resisted.

There is then a logic to Jesus' doctrine, but it is a logic which has never convinced Jews or Judaism.

Let us pass over the fact that the doctrine is unlivable in practice, so unlivable that not even the best Christians practice it. Let us pass over the fact that as an effort at mercy it defeats itself. Suppose your need for your cloak is greater than that of the man who appropriates it, or that someone else requires it more than either of you. Or suppose the slapper is now emboldened to slap other people. Then what you intended for mercy turns out cruelty, increasing the volume of pain in the world.

All these are possible objections to the Christian ideal of nonresistance. But Judaism rejects the counsel of Jesus most basically because it regards it as immoral.

It is unjust that my cloak should be taken away without my consent. It is unjust that I be slapped without provocation. And what is unjust is immoral, what is immoral is never to be acquiesced in, always to be resisted, regardless of its object, even if its object is myself.

The counsel of Judaism, the fourth possible course, is crystal clear. Some of it has already been indicated. Judaism says simply that injustice must never be acquiesced in, no matter who its source and who its object. Justice must always be done; even as it is written:

"Righteousness, ever righteousness, shalt thou pursue."

But it insists also that the justice done shall be pure, as free as possible from hate; it must be a correction of the wrong, not an indulgence in vengefulness.

Therefore it ordains also:

"Thou shalt not bear a grudge nor seek vengeance."

To this end, that justice may be justice, not vindictiveness, Judaism lays down some practical rules.

Thus, it teaches that justice is never a matter of trivialities, but always of substance. It is, for example, not a moral issue that an urchin calls me a name or someone steps on my toe. A wrong has to have size and consequence before cognizance may be taken of it. As lawyers say: *de minimis non curat lex;* the courts and the law do not bother with trifles. The righteous man is easygoing about his prerogatives and acts always on the generous side of his rights.

Even more important in freeing justice from vengefulness is another Jewish prescription. Judaism requires of the one who is wronged that he change places imaginatively with the person who has wronged him. As the rabbis put it:

"Judge not your fellow till you have stood in his place." For once you have done so, two consequences follow, as surely as the night the day:

You will see the injury done you in perspective, in its true size which is always less than your first estimate of it.

And, at the same time, you will come to understand

276

the heart of him who has offended you. Understanding, you will be less likely to hate, certain to hate less, perhaps capable of mercy which is also required of us by Judaism.

Yes, pity by all means, deep, warm, abundant. But—and this is the crux of the matter—never at the expense of the right. Always, always, justice must be done.

This is the theory.

Now for some applications of it.

The first of these is: How are we to behave when we encounter that injustice which is anti-Semitism?

What, for example, are we to do if we find ourselves in the situation of a certain Hebrew schoolteacher and graduate student at a Western university as described by Mr. Norman Cousins sometime ago in a leading editorial of *The Saturday Review of Literature.*

According to Mr. Cousins, at nine o'clock one evening Mr. C., the Hebrew teacher, sat in a coffee shop adjoining the campus, sipping his coffee, reading a book, minding his own business.

Out of a clear sky two university students set about insulting him, uttering coarse anti-Semitic jibes. When these became intolerable, he got up from his place to leave, only to be tripped and set upon. While other students looked on without protest, he was kicked into unconsciousness and so bruised that he was hospitalized for ten days.

Mr. Cousins' purpose in relating this incident is to indict those in the coffee shop who looked on without interfering, the university authorities who took no notice of the incident, the press which played it down, and the police of Iowa City who were remiss in punishing the perpetrators of it.

My point is different. I am concerned with evaluating Mr. C.'s conduct, with the fact that he not only endured the jibes in the coffee shop, but when he came out of the hospital adopted an attitude which can only be characterized as Christian and refused to go to law, continuing in his refusal even when an awakened and indignant public opinion pressed him to do so.

"Everyone," he said, and I am now quoting him, "has the same curse. Nearly everyone in the country feels the same way about the Hebrews. Why then should I prosecute these young men for something that is basically the fault of the country's education system? It's not their fault as much as the fault of the schools, the churches, and the homes."

Here in miniature is the Christian ideal in action. And here its inadequacies stand exposed.

Out of the excess of pity, Mr. C. is being cruel, cruel to the next victims of the hoodlumism he encourages by letting the perpetrators of this hoodlumism go scot-free. Out of moral scruple he is guilty of the immorality of condoning injustice.

How then ought a Jew behave in such a situation?

Not with Christian forbearance such as Mr. C. displayed. Certainly not with instinctive vengefulness, but as befits a Jew with justice as his paramount concern.

278

Let him make sure that the affront is no triviality, that it has substance and consequence.

Let him also look into the minds of the offenders, if he can, to discern whether they are vicious or careless, whether open to reason or closed against it. For, so long as there is any hope of changing them through instruction, that must be his course.

But if, after these precautions, it remains clear that calculated malice is at work, then let him resist to the full, acquiescing in nothing less than total justice, legal and moral.

For nothing less is safe for Jews and for America, nothing less is merciful in the long run, nothing less is moral.

We have traveled a long course, from the consideration of justice between man and man to the Jewish reaction to anti-Semitism. But there is still one final step we must take, the boldest of all, from our present discussion into the realm of theology.

Does this seem too long a step? Then let me point out that justice is justice. If it applies to lesser things, it must apply to greater also. Give me an honest yardstick and I can measure anything with it, myself, my fellows, God Himself.

Him too, the great creative spirit behind the universe.

He causes us to be born without a so much as by your leave, only in the end to take away without our consent the life he has thrust on us.

He has made one of us with a nose too long, a second

with brains too short, a third with a body too fat, and still another with his purse too lean.

He fashions some of us in the shape of round pegs and then drives us into square holes.

He starves the righteous and feasts the wicked.

Too frequently He puts truth on the scaffold, wrong on the throne.

To His injustices as to all others there are three responses.

There is the answer of submissiveness.

Endure, ask no questions, raise no outcry, seek not to change the scheme of things. The proper mood for living is resignation.

This is *miktob,* as the Moslems name it, what is written, fate. It is *Karma,* the wheel of necessity, according to its Brahman name, or *Tao* or *Jen,* according to its Taoist and Confucian. It is Providence, say some Christians and Jews as well.

By this answer and in the name of God, the injustice is tolerated, indeed sanctioned.

There is the second answer. Rebellion. Life is crooked, dishonest. Justice is not in it. Therefore the proper mood for man is to be *b'ragez,* bitter, resentful. And the proper course is to hit back at life, to snatch what one can from it, but never to trust or love it or seek to improve it. So, once again, instinctive vengefulness corrupts the heart and compounds the world's wrongs.

Not bitterness, not submission is the proper Jewish response but the demand for justice, against, in this case, God Himself.

That is why the Jewish tradition, so reverential of God, has also been so *hutspahdik* toward him; that is why the Bible includes the Book of Job, and Hasidism that prayer of the Saint, Levi Yitzhak of Berdichev who, on behalf of justice, challenged the God he revered.

From such challenges to God have sprung some of the greatest advances and deepenings in Jewish theology.

But something more and greater also: the Jewish devotion to social righteousness.

For justice must always be done and if God will not do it then we, if we are true Jews, will undertake to do it for Him and on His behalf.

And so we set about making up for the lapses of the Almighty. But as we do so, and with each triumph over wrong, we come to see with ever greater clarity that injustice is not basic to the scheme of things but a stage in its development for man to transcend. Then we begin to understand how God can still be a God of righteousness, though the world is what it is. For God too is fighting injustice, with us, in us, through us.

In the end, then, we realize that He and we are not opponents, He the injurer and we the injured, but partners in that continuing enterprise of all generations of men of good will; the achievement of that order in which injustice will be no more and righteousness alone prevail.

Out of our resistence to injustice, we arrive at the greatest discovery possible to us as human beings: that He who is the Life of Eternity and we who are but creatures of a brief hour are yet fellows and co-workers in a glorious adventure, the building of the Kingdom of God on earth.

CHAPTER 19

THE SABBATH OF SABBATHS

꙳꙳꙳꙳꙳꙳꙳꙳꙳꙳꙳꙳꙳꙳꙳꙳꙳꙳꙳꙳꙳꙳꙳꙳꙳꙳꙳꙳꙳꙳꙳

A MONG the many names by which Yom Kippur is known in the Hebrew religious calendar, none is stranger than the one which occurs in the Bible, the *Shabbat Shabaton,* the Sabbath of Sabbaths. Despite its Biblical origin, the name is not commonly used, and that, I believe, for an obvious reason: it seems to be peculiarly inappropriate.

A Sabbath is a day of rest, of ease, of relaxation. Whatever else may be said of Yom Kippur, it is not a day of rest. On the contrary, it is by all odds the most strenuous day in the Jewish year.

Aside from the fasting which it requires of us, it is spiritually strenuous. It expects that we shall unearth our sins and those of our world, that we shall atone for them and rededicate ourselves to the good life. To these ends, it sets us reflecting on God, man, and the world, on life and death, on the transiency and frailty of all pursuits, except that of God's will. Whatever else this day may be, it is scarcely a Sabbath.

But, when one stops to think of it, is the weekly Sabbath altogether a Sabbath? To be sure, one abstains from physical labor on that day, one puts worldly care and anxiety from himself, one dresses in his finery, eats well, enjoys the company of his kinsfolk. Yet, as the rabbis pointed out, the day is only half man's—the other half belonging to God.

One is expected not only to be at ease and relax on the Sabbath, but also to worship, to study, to meditate, consciously and deliberately to nurture friendship and love. Let us think of the Sabbath as our parents and grandparents celebrated it, and we will recall that from the moment the housewife kindled the candles and the master of the house went off to Shul, it was a pleasurable but very busy day. Yet—and this is the crux of the matter—all the things with which they were busy were of a peculiar character.

They were first of all, if I may coin a phrase, goal-things, end-things—worship, study, reflection, family love, friendship—the things one worked for all through the week but never had time to enjoy. They were the positive things—self-development, for example, the cultivation of human relations, establishing peace between oneself and God. In sum, they were the things in life that are inherently worth while.

This it is which distinguishes the Sabbath, not, as is commonly supposed, the absence of effort; effort is exacted on the Sabbath, and in impressive quantities. But the effort is exacted for ends, not means, for things positive and not negative, for those interests which are inherently permanent.

Now this misconception as to what constitutes a Sabbath is just one instance of a more general misconception —the error: the error that happiness consists in the elimination of problems.

This error is indeed widespread, especially among young people and the immature old enough to know better.

It seems perfectly natural to a child that because the prince and the princess marry at the end of the fairy tale they will therefore live happily ever after. It never occurs to him that the marriage creates as many problems as it solves, that he who has solved the problem of fulfilling his life has by that very solution created new problems, ranging all the way from household budgets and the training of children, to keeping alive the love that created the marriage in the first place.

Again, who has not heard some young person exclaim: "If only I had this or that, or could solve this or that problem, I would not ask another thing." Only a young person could say this. Older people, more experienced, know better. They know that when the one supposedly crucial problem is solved, others will arise that in their way will seem no less crucial and pressing. Indeed, as in the case of marriage, the very solution of the problem itself opens up new problems.

This notion, that problems can be eliminated, and that happiness consists in their elimination, I have called the error of youth, or of the immature, those who are grown up chronologically, but not spiritually. And indeed, there is no better test of maturity than this—the realism of a person's expectations as to problems and their solution.

It is an error for people to count on being problem free. There is no such thing in life. Moreover, it is a dangerous error, for it is an open invitation to disillusionment. One is forever expecting too much, forever being disappointed, until disappointment becomes a general and constant mood.

I can vividly recall one perpetual adolescent of this sort.

When I met him first on a preaching visit to Indianapolis, back in 1926, he was in the throes of a star-crossed love affair, and on first acquaintance assured me passionately that if only his parents would withdraw their opposition to his marriage, his bliss would be undying.

I met him next in 1928 when, already married, he expressed unhappiness over the fact that his business, though moderately successful, was not yielding him the quick wealth which was coming to so many of his associates. Two years later, in 1930, he was in despair lest the depression wipe him out altogether. If only he could keep his head above water, he would ask nothing else out of life.

Three years later, when I left Indianapolis, he had not only survived the depression, but was in the relatively unique position of having prospered during it. But now a new problem weighed on him. He was not by birth one of the socially acceptable. If only he, and, even more, his wife and children, could make their way into that charmed circle. . . .

In 1939 I visited Indianapolis and caught a quick glimpse of him in the audience I was addressing. He was simply redolent with prosperity; his wife and children sat to his right, and to his left sat one of the most acceptable of all the social acceptables of the community.

He had made wish after wish, and as though he owned the magic ring, every wish had been granted. But was he content?

Three years ago I met him in the club car of a train. I have never seen a more restless human being: restless about his marriage, his family, his business, his entire life. In each area of his being, he complained, there were problems—problems with his children, with his employees, with his wife. It was disheartening, he insisted, that a man should struggle as he had done, and in the end find himself so beset. He described himself as tired, discouraged, bored.

I offer him to you as an illustration of both the error and its consequences.

But what, you will say, is the alternative? Are we doomed to go forever from one problem to the next, without gain, advance, or progress? Are we caught on a treadmill?

That we are made to go from one problem to the next—that I believe is our destiny.

The process, however, is not futile and unprogressive. On the contrary it can represent a steady gain.

Let me return to our first reflections.

Not even the Sabbath of Sabbaths, we discovered, is an effortless day. What makes it the Sabbath is not the absence of problems but the fact that its problems are all positive, constructive, ends in themselves, inherently worth while. And this is progress in life—to keep on forever transcending its negative issues, to keep oneself increasingly occupied with its positive.

And how can one tell which are negative activities? By a very simple test, by whether they are inherently worth while, by whether one would engage in them for their own sake.

Keeping well is one such a negative activity. Who would want to get sick just so that he might have an occasion to get well again? Making money is another such negative activity. Who would want to live in order to make a living?

On the other hand, friendship, love, education, social service—these are all positive activities, things worth while for their own sake. To be sure they have the value of being instruments too. Nonetheless,

One does live to have friends and cultivate them,
One does live to undergo the experience of love,
One does live to know, to think, to dream, to aspire,
One does live to serve mankind.

Do you want then a simple test of whether your life is getting anywhere? Do not ask yourself whether you are becoming problem free. Ask rather whether the proportion of inherently worth-while problems in your existence is mounting over those that are negative and instrumental.

The Western world has created two great epics of the next world—*The Divine Comedy* and *Paradise Lost*. Both Dante and Milton in describing Heaven slipped into the common error which I am discussing. Each of them portrayed it as a place where there are no problems, where existence is effortless. The result is that life in Heaven as they picture it is so much a bore that Hell seems inviting by contrast. Even the poets were bored with their notions of Heaven, otherwise why should both of them have written so much better verse in describing Hell? For the fact is that Dante's *Inferno* is as literature better than his *Paradiso,* and Milton's *Paradise Lost* far outstrips his *Paradise Regained.*

The ancient rabbis may have been as naïve as Dante and Milton in their imaginings of the next world, but they were much wiser about human nature. They knew men too well to suppose that they would be happy doing nothing and being problem free.

No, in their description of eternal bliss, the souls of the blessed are described as being very busy, and as having plenty of problems. They contemplate and seek to comprehend the infinite mystery of God's being. They study Torah in adult classes. They perform the *Mitzvoth*—at least the more spiritual *Mitzvoth.* And they take an active interest in the still unfinished career of man on earth, in his struggle for goodness and truth.

This, say the rabbis, is really Heaven; not to be without problems but to have all one's problems positive, inherently worth while, ends in themselves.

It is in this spirit, too, that I envisage my utopia on earth. When I look into the human future I see scientists still struggling with problems, but they are the problems of wresting the truth from nature, not of wasting time fighting for freedom of the intellect. I see artists still working day and night at their canvases and marble, but to incarnate their vision of beauty, not to keep the wolves from their doors. I see all men laboring not to ward off hunger, disease, and enslavement, but for self-fulfillment and mutual aid. I see each religion and culture exerting its fullest energies but for the purpose not of fighting off the assault of other faiths and traditions but so as to make the most of its own resources for its own sake and that of the world. I see each polity, each economy hard at work but with one problem only—to give to each person the maximum of freedom, the most generous access to the good things of living. I see each national state very very busy not in defending itself against its neighbors but in doing its best for its citizens and its sister national states.

This to me will be heaven on earth. This is the direction in which all of us must move—toward a Sabbath of Sabbaths which like this day is not problem free but which rather frees us for those problems which are inherently affirmative and precious, the problems in which life finds meaning.

CHAPTER 20

THE FEAR OF LIFE

❈❈❈❈❈❈❈❈❈❈❈❈❈❈❈❈❈❈❈❈❈❈❈❈❈❈❈❈❈❈

O F ALL the names assigned by our ancestors to the High Holidays of Rosh Hashanah and Yom Kippur, none is more curious and yet more revealing than the name *Yomim Noraim*. For our forefathers never spoke of this solemn season as the High Holidays. They always called them Yomim Noraim, or Days of Fear. And no Jew who enters the synagogue on those days with an open heart and sensitive soul can fail to understand the psychology of this curious name. For Rosh Hashanah and Yom Kippur are in a real sense just what our ancestors called them—Days of Fear.

As we sit in the synagogue at the end of one year and the beginning of another, contemplating the past and facing the future, what strange and awful terrors beset us. From day to day we have been content to live on, unquestioning and unreflecting; but on this day of all days, deep in our hearts lies a haunting challenge. Who knows what the year to come will bring? Who knows what strange and awful sorrow may befall us in the twelve months which lie ahead? Over us on this day hangs a dark pall of fear. For the future behind its inscrutable veil holds many things. To one of us it may bring death, to another sickness, to a third the agony of bereavement, and still to another the cold hand of poverty. And when we consider what cruel things the future may inflict on us in our weakness we grow afraid, and call these hours the hours of the Days of Fear.

We are all of us afraid, today. Afraid of life and the hard things it can do to us. And I should be derelict in my duty if I did not bring to light the hidden fears of your hearts, and tell you how you may perhaps overcome them.

To live and to be afraid are the same thing. Every living creature from the humblest insect to man knows the meaning of fear. For among all the ingredients compounded in the creation of life, fear is one of the most important. The savage in the jungle has his fears. He dreads the wild beasts, the sword of his enemy, and the magic of those who hate him. And civilized man, though the nature of his fears has changed, is still like his more primitive brother, a creature of timidities.

All of us want the good things of life, the vibrancy of health, the security of wealth, the comfort of ease, the solace of love, and the inspiration of beauty. But the cup of life runs bitter as well as sweet, and the world gives us not only the pleasant things that we want, but the horrible and cruel things in infinite variety from which we shrink. And because we know the bitter things that fate can do to us, we are afraid to live. In this respect we are less fortunate than the animal or the savage. Primitive man may have his fears, but they are the fears of present evils, while we have our fears plus the imagination. And it is this com•bination which makes cowards of us all, for it raises the recognition not only of real evils, but also the ghosts of evils not yet born.

I say that most modern men are afraid of life just because they have the capacity for visualizing the future. We fear for our children just because we know into what strange paths they may wander. We are timorous about our health because we can picture ourselves in the grasp of strange, malignant diseases. We fret about the security of our position because we know how slight an error may ruin our standing with others. And we dread for our wealth because we can visualize ourselves in the hard lot of privation and poverty, because we can imagine ourselves stripped of the hard-earned things which we now possess.

In short, we are afraid of life and its naked, cruel realities. Civilized man is infinitely stronger than any other living thing; but on his spirit has come that cancerous growth of worry, timidity, and uncertainty which I have characterized as the Fear of Life.

It is an elementary law of all living things that what we are afraid of we run away from. And man in his fear of life tries to escape it. We sometimes do not realize how much our conduct is an attempt to escape from this fear of living. Those who can, take flight in an actual withdrawal from participation in life. The monk in the monastery sits in solitude all his life because thereby he feels secure from the evils of the world. The world is a strenuous place in which to live, a place of smoke and sweat, of noise and turmoil.

It is a place in which one may meet with poverty and temptation. And so men take refuge in their cells where there are no poverties and no hungers, where one is secure from all evil allurements, where one may escape from life. And not unlike the monk in his cell is the scholar in his ivory tower.

But flight from life because of cowardice is not confined to the monk and the scholar. The man who chooses an easier profession because it offers security rather than the adventure of a more difficult task, the person who sees wrong in the world and refuses to raise the voice of protest because of the consequences—all these are cowards fleeing from the dread of life.

There is another, more interesting way of playing the coward from fear than by withdrawal from life, and that is escape through the mind. People like to build up pleasant illusions about themselves and the world; illusions more comforting than reality. In these they wrap themselves as in a protecting blanket against the hard realities. The American Indian, afraid of the hardness of his life, invented the dream of a happy hunting-ground where his enemies would vex him no more and where there was always game for his arrow. And when life became too difficult, the Indian would tell himself of the pleasant days that awaited him in the next world.

Psychologists tell us that one of the most dangerous of modern phenomena is the tendency to have recourse to a dream life. The weak and the cowardly, unable to fight life's battles, build for themselves imaginary worlds in which they live. They compensate for what life does not give them by imagining themselves as they should like to be. The obscure person dreams of himself as prominent in society. The coward indulges in day dreams in which he plays the hero.

Hard experience has taught promoters of motion pictures that every movie must have a happy ending to be successful. In everyday life things do not always end as we should like them to. Virtue does not always prevail and things very seldom turn out quite in accordance with our hearts' desire. It is because the theater is in essence an expression of the fear of life, and the escape from it, that the fade-out must always find the heroine happily united with the hero; otherwise the audience tends to feel itself cheated. It came to the theater to escape life's problems and it will not have life's disappointing realities thrust back upon it.

The fear of life, and the escape from it—these, then, are never-failing motifs of human action. And yet, there is something in man which makes him feel that it is undignified to be afraid of this business of living, that it is cowardly to attempt to escape. It was Gilbert K. Chesterton who made one of his characters say, "No man can call himself a man as long as there is anything in the universe of which he is afraid." The fear of the future is not only undignified, but it is also one of the most futile emotions that dominate man. For, try as he will, no human being can escape the hard realities of the world as it is, and no attempt to escape ever brings peace. A cowardly attitude toward life, as Shakespeare once put it, makes cowards of us all, and cowards die many times. There is no man less happy than the refugee from life.

There comes a time when every man grows weary of his illusions. When he rises in rebellion against them, when he insists on looking at life as it really is, and when he refuses to delude himself any further by a fearful contemplation of reality through the rosy spectacles of his dreams. At such times all of us want to live boldly and unafraid, facing the world without fear of the morrow, and without the cringing which at other times leads us to attempt to escape.

Where shall we gather the strength and courage for this? In days when life has made cowards of us all, how can we cultivate the capacity to live resolutely?

Some men have done it. Some men have stood face to face with the hardest of realities and have been strong enough to be courageous about life. In the Book of Daniel there is found the tale of the three men who refused to bow down to Nebuchadnezzar's idol. And when he threatened them with death in a fiery furnace, and asked who it was that could save them from his royal wrath, they said:

"O Nebuchadnezzar, we have no need to answer thee. If our God whom we serve is able to deliver us He will deliver us from the burning, fiery furnace and out of thy hand. And if not, be it known to thee, O king, that we will not serve thy gods nor worship the image which thou hast set up." Here is courage in the face of the evil powers of the world.

Robert Louis Stevenson, who wrote those lovely children's poems recited in every nursery, and who was the author of *Aes Triplex,* the greatest essay ever written in English on the subject of courage—would anyone dream that he wrote these things as he lay dying for fourteen years in Samoa, far from his friends? Here was a man to whom the realities of life had been infinitely hard, who had every reason to be afraid of life and to attempt to escape from it; and yet—let me quote a passage from a letter of his, to show what courage really is:

"For fourteen years I have not had a day's real health; I have awakened sick and gone to bed weary; and I have done my work unflinchingly. I have written in bed, and written out of it, written in haemorrhages, written in sickness, written torn by coughing, written when my head swam for weakness; and for so long, it seems to me I have won my wager and recovered my glove. And the battle goes on—ill or well is a trifle, so as it goes. I was made for a contest, and the Powers have so willed that my battlefield should be this dingy, inglorious one of the bed and the physic bottle. At least I have not failed, but I would have preferred a place of trumpeting and the open air above my head."

And the question which we ask ourselves as we read of these examples of courage is: How can we attain to the wisdom of these heroes? How can we rise above the degrading fear which makes us cowards of life and refugees from it? What is the secret of strength in the hour of darkness and evil? How can we, too, live boldly?

There are three steps to courage. Three roads which one must follow before he can be free from the fear of life.

The first is the road of disillusionment. There is no harder word than disillusionment. It connotes the blasting of hopes and dreams, and yet I say that before one can live courageously he must learn to cultivate disillusionment. For the opposite of disillusionment is illusion, and no one can live truthfully and boldly so long as he conceals the realities by a wall of illusion which he fears to penetrate because of his dread of life. Stevenson did not delude himself, nor did the three Jews before Nebuchadnezzar fool themselves as to the gravity of their crisis. The first step toward courage involves the stripping off of illusion. Let us learn to shatter our daydreams and fantasies that we find so comforting.

Let us steel ourselves to see life steady and to see it whole. Let us learn what it really is in all its nakedness and cruelty. If it be a cruel monster without compassion or mercy, let us know that first. Then at least we shall have realized the worst and have prepared ourselves for it. The man who expects the worst need have no fears; he is prepared. And when we have ceased to comfort and beguile ourselves with fantasies and illusions, we shall have attained the first step toward the attainment of manhood. Only he is a grown man who knows and admits, who acknowledges and is reconciled to the fact that human beings do not live in a fool's paradise.

Having traversed the path of disillusionment, we must now tread the second road, the road of duty. Each of us has a task in life. The scientist has his search for the proof, the mother her baby, the poet his song, the ditchdigger his ditch and the merchant his business. None of us can control life. It is much too strong for us. It can do all sorts of strange and horrible things to us. But one thing it cannot do. It cannot take from us the task and the duty which it itself imposed upon us. It cannot make the three Jews

297

standing before Nebuchadnezzar worship any other God but the true God. It could not make Stevenson cease to write his poetry. And we can say to this strange specter called life: "I am powerless before you. You hold me in the hollow of your hand. You can strip me of everything I have. But one thing you cannot take from me, my duty and task in life. That is mine eternally."

There is a beautiful tale in the Talmud about the Emperor Hadrian and the old Jew whom he found planting trees. The Emperor in astonishment said to the aged Jew, "Old man, these trees will not give fruit for another twenty years; do you expect to be alive to eat the fruit of your labor?" And the old man replied: "If God wills, I shall eat; and if not, my father and his father before me planted trees for me. It is my duty, then, to provide for those who shall come after me."

That is why we need not fear life—because our duty and its fulfillment none can take from us. Nay, more, none can ask from us more than that we fulfill our obligations as we see them. Wherefore, let the mother tend her young, and let the poet sing his song, and the laborer dig his ditch, and let the merchant do his best; and if life is hard, and the child grows into an ungrateful man and goes astray, and the poet's song falls on deaf ears, and the laborer digs his ditch in vain, and the merchant fails in his business endeavors—then at least each in turn will have done his duty. His hands are clean. He can say with Horace, *"Integer vitae scelerisque purus*—he who is whole in his life and clean from sin need not fear the future."

Of the courage which comes from one's duty done I

could give illustrations from some of mankind's greatest souls; but the most beautiful illustration I know of is found in the simple Latin inscription left by a simple Roman woman who lived over 2,000 years ago. Here is what she says: "Stranger, I have only a little to say. Stop and read. This is the grave of a not too beautiful woman. I loved my husband with all my heart. I gave birth to two sons. One I leave behind me alive, the other I buried in his youth. I served my household, I spun my wool, I tended my hearth. *Dixi. Abi*—I have spoken. You may depart."

What a wealth of quiet dignity in these simple words of a simple woman. This is living with courage. This is the secret of the escape from the fear of life. Not illusion, comforting but false, but a fulfillment of one's task in life, as best one may.

And then, there is the third road. The road of faith and hope. The road which leads us to the realization that in the fulfillment of our duty lies the will of God. That the good we do is treasured eternally in the divine scheme of things. That out of our infinitely small duties God weaves for Himself on the loom of time a new heaven and a new earth. The road of faith which teaches that God has so ordered the world that from the good deeds fulfilled courageously in the hour of sorrow there will come at the end of days a new mankind which will have less cause than we to be afraid of life because the world will be kinder and better than it is now.

It was Josiah Royce, the great American philosopher, who once said: "Endurance is the measure of a man." And to those of you who fear for tomorrow's bread, to those who during the last year have watched their worldly goods slip away from them, to all that carry within them secret fears, the message of Judaism is that no one can do any more than his duty in the spirit of faith and truth. Wherefore, face the year with courage, in the spirit of that ancient wisdom of Hillel:

"When none has the courage to be a man, stand thou up and be one."

CHAPTER 21

REMEMBER US UNTO LIFE

ALL THROUGH our Rosh Hashanah worship one traditional prayer echoes and re-echoes—the prayer for life:
"Remember us unto life, O King who delightest in life."

And yet, even as we pray for life, we know that it is
more than life that we want. For the mere fact of physical
existence is not an end in itself. Each of us can envisage
circumstances under which life would be a burden to him
—the loss of faculties, bereavement of those whom one
loves most deeply, enslavement to the will of others. Not
life alone, but life with a plus: that is the real purport of
our worship. When we reflect on what that plus is, we
may have our difficulties in defining its character. Serenity,
peace of spirit, a sense of joy—these are certainly elements
in the whole. Security, a reasonable confidence that one is
protected against the hazards which threaten human existence, this is perhaps another element. Perhaps the whole
thing can be caught by saying that we want in addition to
living a sense of the worthwhileness of our existence—that
sense of the worthwhileness of our existence which we
know as happiness.

And yet, these are just the qualities of living which are denied to us in the present juncture of human affairs. No one can be serene in spirit in these days. Even if he is himself untouched by the world catastrophe, his imagination, his sympathy with the millions who suffer make peace of heart impossible. Security, too, is something which is denied us. No one can foreread the future. There are no sure guards against the threats of evil contingencies. This is the cruel and tragic impasse of our generation. Here we are, living our lives without the very things which make life worth while, and with little assurance that these things will be available to us in the immediate future.

By a coincidence that is not quite coincidence, the prophetic lesson for the second day of Rosh Hashanah is drawn from the prophecies of Jeremiah. Of all Scriptural figures Jeremiah, the prophet of Anathoth, is closest to us. Like us he lived in a period of chaos, at a time when a great military empire had arisen in Babylonia to threaten the whole world. With his eyes he witnessed the dark shadow of Babylonia spread over his native land. Personal happiness was not his. He was indeed a Man of Sorrows. Nor was security his lot. His career was marked by none of the qualities which we normally regard as the necessary plus to life. And yet he lived, and lived creatively and long. Perhaps in his precedent we who must also live without peace of mind and security can find some guidance for ourselves.

On what did Jeremiah live? On duty. From birth he felt himself dedicated to the achievement of certain obligations. "Before I formed thee in the belly, I knew thee. Before thou didst come forth from the womb, I had consecrated thee." This sense of duty in him, according to his own testimony, was in his heart as a burning fire. In other words, he inverted the pyramid of life. Whereas we are likely to feel that our purpose in living is happiness and security, he made his goal the fulfillment of what he regarded as his duty.

These are hard times. They call for a hard, stern doctrine. And the doctrine amounts to this: that we must stop demanding from life that we shall be happy and secure, and live for what is our duty. Such a course is, in the first place, the part of wisdom. We cannot have happiness and security even if we insist on them. Nor have we any particular claim to these qualities in our life. Indeed, much that is wrong with the tone and tenor of Western society springs from the tendency to demand from life that it shall make us happy. The weakness of democracy has in great measure been exposed as lying just on this point. Men insist that democracy shall give them what they want of life. If, therefore, it does not accede to their demands, they are done with it. They are conscious of what society owes them and forgetful of what they owe it.

To live for duty, this is the message of Jeremiah. It is indeed the message of the whole Jewish tradition which insists that man lives to fulfill the will of God as expressed in the *Mitzvoth* or Commandments. It is the testimony of nature written into the structure of the human body. For nature has not invested us with physical shells for security. There is no lobe in our brain, no auricle or ventricle in our heart, which is our organ of happiness. The faculties with which we have been invested by nature are those of thought and action. And it is interesting to observe, as Bergson points out, that it is just these, thought and action, that are treasured by nature. When one of the higher mammals undergoes starvation, it is the nerve system which yields last. And in the psychological process of amnesia, of progressive and accumulated loss of memory, it is the verbs, the words of action, which hold on most tenaciously.

But duty is a vague and elusive word. What is the duty of man? That too is written both in Scripture and in nature. It is recorded in Scripture that each man is God in miniature, that it is his life mission to achieve knowledge, justice, and mercy, to treat with all human beings as incarnations of the Divine, and to win for them the right to the truth, the enjoyment of justice, and the experience of mercy. These same goals are prescribed by nature itself. For when one looks back over the evolution of life, one perceives that its progress has been from insensitivity toward thought, from bondage to the trammels of time, space, cause and effect toward freedom, from brutality to insight. The life of reason, the love of freedom, the life of insights: the embodiment of these in our own existence, the translation of these to society—this is the mission of man. This then is our duty when one world is dying and a new world is being born. To preserve whatever of truth, freedom, and mercy has been achieved among men by the past and to shape the new world for their enlargement. More specifically, that means in America a fuller democracy, a richer and more abundant life for all, a greater measure of economic justice. This is how we must comport ourselves in this hour of tragic crisis. We must stop insisting on security and happiness for ourselves and give our lives to what are our transparent duties as recorded in Scripture and in the testament of life. And if we do so, by a strange and bizarre paradox, we may achieve a kind of happiness and security. That happiness and security, in spite of his own unhappiness and insecurity, Jeremiah achieved. For this is the paradox of happiness—it is not to be attained by seeking it. It is a by-product of the fulfillment of duty, of the realization of function. Seek happiness and it will elude you. Forget it and you may attain it. And this is the paradox of security. No one can build walls against danger strong enough for any contingency. The securest person is the one who does not fortify himself but who exposes himself completely to all things.

CHAPTER 22

IF MAN IS GOD

PHARAOH, as portrayed in the Book of Exodus, is a brutal, wanton, and cynical tyrant, altogether insensitive to the demands of equity. But he is a human being. Not even he lays claim to a more exalted station.

Pharaoh, as the rabbis envisaged him, is a more sinister figure—not alone because their imagination invested him with even more desperate cruelties than those which Scripture lists, but especially because of his opinion of himself. For in their portrayal he is man asserting to be greater than man, to be no less than God.

This notion of the king who arrogates the attributes of divinity to himself is no vagary of the ancient Jewish mind. It represents in part a consequence of prophetic vehemence in style and attitude—witness the characterization of the King of Assyria by Isaiah, and more specifically, Ezekiel's description of the Pharaoh of his own day:

"Thus saith the Lord God, Behold I am against thee, Pharaoh King of Egypt, the great dragon that lieth in the midst of his rivers, which hath said, 'My river is my own and I have made it for myself.' "

Even more decisive than prophetic utterance in the fram-
ing of the notion of the Man-God, and doubtless the factual
base for it was a political reality of ancient paganism. For
in all actuality kings and emperors asserted themselves to
be gods and were so regarded. Such were the pretenses of
the Pharaohs, the Hellenistic emperors, the Seleucids, the
Ptolemies, and the Caesars of Rome. It is difficult to determine how seriously royal assertions of divinity were taken.
To those at the head of states the claim must have been no
more than a matter of *Realpolitik,* and there was no little
banter over the matter among sophisticates, such as the
Roman satirists. But regardless of the earnestness or lack
of it with which the doctrine was regarded, there could be
no question as to what it implied.

When rulers insisted that they were manifest gods, they
meant by their insistence, first, that there was no law superior to their will; second, that as gods they recognized
no indebtedness for their privileges and powers, and con-
sequently were free to employ them as they saw fit; and
third, that there was no larger authority to which either the
emperor or the state owed obedience.

It was these corollaries which, for the rabbis, translated
a blasphemous unintelligibility into a specific doctrine to
be stoutly resisted. For to them God was God. To be sure,
they regarded all men as partaking of God's character. In
that fact, the individual was invested with dignity and
deathlessness, his aspirations, as manifestations of cosmic
aspiration, took on meaning and permanence beyond his
own existence. But participation in divinity was to them a
privilege which each person shared with all others, even to

307

some extent with animals and brute matter. As a shared experience it was something to be lived out co-operatively with all other objectifications of the divine essence. What is more, partaking of divinity was never complete in any single individual. If one was little lower than the angels, he was still in body, in mind, in heart, a frail human—who as such ought subdue his will to conformity with that of God. In consequence, every man, even the most exalted, was subject to God's law, was indebted to God for his talents and owed it to God to use them for the attainment of over-arching divinely set goals.

Until recently there was no occasion for modern men to regard the caprices of ancient rulers as more than outmoded and grotesque self-inflation. Of late there has been less occasion to be condescending toward the concept of the Man-God. For, as is painfully evident, dictators have taken to talking with the same overweening arrogance with which once the Pharaohs and Caesars characterized themselves. The idea of Man-God has in our age been exhibited too frequently and has been attended by too much destructiveness to permit of light dismissal.

But what is less often perceived is that the dictator represents, except in degree of power and malevolence, no unique expression of the modern temper. For to the extent to which the mechanistic, materialistic philosophy has come to dominate the thought processes of men, to that extent all men even if they are devoid of political station are invited to Caesarism. Given the irreligious interpretation of reality, the attitude that a vast pointlessness lies at the core of all that is, and moral principles must come to be regarded as figments of the physicochemical processes of the human organism. Since the gifts of the universe are the flotsam and jetsam of senseless cosmic tides, the individual finds himself under no obligation as to their use. Nor is there any ground for subordinating oneself to objectives larger than the self, in view of the general purposelessness of all things.

Now as in ages past there are only two alternatives. Either God is God, or he is not. If God be God, then man is man, dignified by his participation in the divine essence, finding guidance for conduct in the divine will, and purposiveness in the divine purpose, but he is still human, still subject to the Kingship of God. If there is no God, man becomes God *faute de mieux*.

Religion subserves many purposes. It is a principle of explanation of the universe, in the light of which the individual can find meaning for his own career and that of mankind. It is a sanction for morality. It is an esthetic, and much else besides. But not the least of its utilities is this: by positing God it inhibits man from laying claim to being God. It prevents his becoming less than man through the arrogance of claiming to be more. In brief, it helps to keep man human.

CHAPTER 23

TO HOLD WITH OPEN ARMS

✹✹✹✹✹✹✹✹✹✹✹✹✹✹✹✹✹✹✹✹✹✹✹✹✹✹✹✹✹✹✹✹

I T IS A sound convention which requires that a sermon begin with a text—some verse from Scripture, or from Rabbinic literature, which summarizes the theme. But it is well to understand that a text is, after all, only the soul-experience of some man boiled down to the size of an epigram. At some time in the past a prophet or a saint met God, wrestled with good or evil, tasted of life and found it bitter or sweet, contemplated death, and then distilled the adventure into a single line, for those that would come after him. That is a text.

But it is not only the great, the saints, the prophets, and the heroes who contemplate God, life, and death. We, too, the plainer folk of the world, live, love, laugh, and suffer, and by no means always on the surface. We, too, catch glimpses of eternity and the things that people do. Not only of Moses, but of us, too, it may be said, as Lowell put it:

> *Daily with souls that cringe and plot*
> *We Sinais climb and know it not.*

There are texts in us, too, in our commonplace experiences, if only we are wise enough to discern them.

One such experience, a *textual* experience, so to speak, fell to my lot not so long ago. There was nothing dramatic about its setting nor unusual in its circumstances. And yet to me it was a moment of discovery, almost of revelation.

Let me recount it very briefly, as befits a text. After a long illness, I was permitted for the first time to step out of doors. And, as I crossed the threshold, sunlight greeted me. This is my experience—all there is to it. And yet, so long as I live, I shall never forget that moment. It was mid-January—a time of cold and storm up north, but in Texas, where I happened to be, a season much like our spring. The sky overhead was very blue, very clear, and very, very high. Not, I thought, the *shamayim*, heaven, but *shemei shamayim*, a heaven of heavens. A faint wind blew from off the western plains, cool and yet somehow tinged with warmth—like a dry chilled wine. And everywhere in the firmament above me, in the great vault between earth and sky, on the pavements, the buildings—the golden glow of the sunlight. It touched me, too, with friendship, with warmth, with blessing. And as I basked in its glory there ran through my mind those wonder words of the prophet about the sun which someday shall rise with healing on its wings.

In that instant I looked about me to see whether anyone else showed on his face the joy, almost the beatitude, I felt. But no, there they walked—men and women and children, in the glory of a golden flood, and so far as I could detect, there was none to give it heed. And then I remembered how often, I, too, had been indifferent to sunlight, how often, preoccupied with petty and sometimes mean concerns, I had disregarded it. And I said to myself—how precious is the sunlight but alas, how careless of it are men. How precious—how careless. This has been a refrain sounding in me ever since.

It rang in my spirit when I entered my own home again after months of absence, when I heard from a nearby room the excited voices of my children at play; when I looked once more on the dear faces of some of my friends; when I was able for the first time to speak again from my pulpit in the name of our faith and tradition, to join in worship of the God who gives us so much of which we are so careless.

And a resolution crystallized within me. I said to myself that at the very first opportunity I would speak of this. I knew full well that it is a commonplace truth, that there is nothing clever about my private rediscovery of it, nothing ingenious about my way of putting it. But I was not interested in being original or clever or ingenious. I wanted only to remind my listeners, as I was reminded, to spend life wisely, not to squander it.

I wanted to say to the husbands and wives who love one another: "How precious is your lot in that it is one of love. Do not be, even for a moment, casual with your good fortune. Love one another while yet you may."

And to parents: "How precious is the gift of your children. Never, never be too busy for the wonder and miracle of them. They will be grown up soon enough and grown away, too."

We human beings, we frail reeds who are yet, as Pascal

said, *thinking* reeds, *feeling* reeds, how precious are our endowments—minds to know, eyes to see, ears to listen, hearts to stir with pity, and to dream of justice and of a perfected world. How often are we indifferent to all these!

And we who are Jews and Americans, heirs of two great traditions, how fortunate our lot in both, and how blind we are to our double good fortune.

This is what struggled in me for utterance—as it struggled in Edna St. Vincent Millay when she cried out:

"O world I cannot hold thee close enough."

I want to urge myself and all others to hold the world tight—to embrace life with all our hearts and all our souls and all our might. For it is precious, ineffably precious, and we are careless, wantonly careless of it.

And yet, when I first resolved to express all this, I knew that it was only a half truth.

Could I have retained the sunlight no matter how hard I tried? Could I have prevented the sun from setting? Could I have kept even my own eyes from becoming satiated and bored with the glory of the day? That moment had to slip away. And had I tried to hold on to it, what would I have achieved? It would have gone from me in any case. And I would have been left disconsolate, embittered, convinced that I had been cheated.

But it is not only the sunlight that must slip away—our youth goes also, our years, our children, our senses, our lives. This is the nature of things, an inevitability. And the sooner we make our peace with it the better. Did I urge myself a moment ago to hold on? I would have done better, it now begins to appear, to have preached the opposite doctrine of letting go—the doctrine of Socrates who called life a *peisithanatos*—a persuader of death, a teacher of the art of relinquishing. It was the doctrine of Goethe who said: *Entsagen sollst, du sollst entsagen*—Thou shalt renounce. And it was the doctrine of the ancient rabbis who despite their love of life said: He who would die let him hold on to life.

It is a sound doctrine.

First because, as we have just seen, it makes peace with inevitability. And the inevitable is something with which everyone should be at peace. Second, because nothing can be more grotesque and more undignified than a futile attempt to hold on.

Let us think of the men and women who cannot grow old gracefully because they cling too hard to a youth that is escaping them; of the parents who cannot let their children go free to live their own lives; of the people who in times of general calamity have only themselves in mind.

What is it that drives people to such unseemly conduct, to such flagrant selfishness except the attitude which I have just commended—a vigorous holding on to life? Besides, are there not times when one ought hold life cheap, as something to be lightly surrendered? In defense of one's country, for example, in the service of truth, justice, and mercy, in the advancement of mankind?

This, then, is the great truth of human existence. One must not hold life too precious. One must always be prepared to let it go.

And now we are indeed confused. First we learn that

life is a privilege—cling to it! Then we are instructed: Thou shalt renounce!

A paradox, and a self-contradiction! But neither the paradox nor the contradiction are of my making. They are a law written into the scheme of things—that a man must hold his existence dear and cheap at the same time.

Is it not, then, an impossible assignment to which destiny has set us? It does not ask of us that we hold life dear at one moment, and cheap at the next, but that we do both simultaneously. Now I can grasp something in my fist or let my hand lie open. I can clasp it to my breast or hold it at arm's length. I can embrace it, enfolding it in my arms, or let my arms hang loose. But how can I be expected to do both at once?

To which the answer is: With your body, of course not. But with your spirit, why not?

Is one not forever doing paradoxical and mutually contradictory things in his soul?

One wears his mind out in study, and yet has more mind with which to study. One gives away his heart in love and yet has more heart to give away. One perishes out of pity for a suffering world, and is the stronger therefor.

So, too, it is possible at one and the same time to hold on to life and let it go provided—well let me put it this way:

We are involved in a tug of war: Here on the left, is the necessity to renounce life and all it contains. Here on the right, the yearning to affirm it and its experiences. And between these two is a terrible tension, for they pull in opposite directions.

But suppose that here in the center I introduce a third force, one that lifts upward. My two irreconcilables now swing together, both pulling down against the new element. And the harder they pull, the closer together they come.

God is the third element, that new force that resolves the terrible contradiction, the intolerable tension of life.

And for this purpose it does not especially matter how we conceive God. I have been a great zealot for a mature idea of God. I have urged again and again that we think through our theology, not limping along on a child's notion of God as an old man in the sky. But for my immediate purpose, all of this is irrelevant. What is relevant is this: that so soon as a man believes in God, so soon indeed as he wills to believe in Him, the terrible strain is eased; nay, it disappears, and that for two reasons.

In the first place, because a new and higher purpose is introduced into life, the purpose of doing the will of God, to put it in Jewish terms, of performing the *Mitzvoth*. This now becomes the reason for our existence. We are soldiers whose commander has stationed them at a post. How we like our assignment, whether we feel inclined to cling to it, or to let it go, is an irrelevant issue. Our hands are too busy with our duties to be either embracing the world or pushing it away.

That is why it is written: "Make thy will conform to His, then His will be thine, and all things will be as thou desirest."

But that, it might be urged, only evades the problem. By concentrating on duty we forget the conflicting drives

316

within ourselves. The truth is, however, that, given God,
the problem is solved not only by evasion but directly; that
it is solved, curiously enough, by being made more intense.
For, given God, everything becomes more precious, more
to be loved and clung to, more embraceable; and yet at the
same time easier to give up.

Given God, everything becomes more precious.

That sunshine in Dallas was not a chance effect, a lucky
accident. It was an effect created by a great Artist, the
Master Painter of Eternity. And because it came from
God's brush it is more valuable even than I had at first
conceived.

And the laughter of children, precious in itself, becomes
infinitely more precious because the joy of the cosmos is
in it.

And the sweetness of our friends' faces is dearer because
these are fragments of an infinite sweetness.

All of life is the more treasurable because a great and
Holy Spirit is in it.

And yet, it is easier for me to let go.

For these things are not and never have been mine. They
belong to the Universe and the God who stands behind it.
True, I have been privileged to enjoy them for an hour but
they were always a loan due to be recalled.

And I let go of them the more easily because I know
that as parts of the divine economy they will not be lost.
The sunset, the bird's song, the baby's smile, the thunder
of music, the surge of great poetry, the dreams of the heart,
and my own being, dear to me as every man's is to him,
all these I can well trust to Him who made them. There

is poignancy and regret about giving them up, but no anxiety. When they slip from my hands they will pass to hands better, stronger, and wiser than mine.

This then is the insight which came to me as I stood some months ago in a blaze of sunlight: Life is dear, let us then hold it tight while we yet may; but we must hold it loosely also!

And only with God can we ease the intolerable tension of our existence. For only when He is given, can we hold life at once infinitely precious and yet as a thing lightly to be surrendered. Only because of Him is it made possible for us to clasp the world, but with relaxed hands; to embrace it, but with open arms.